# Ikigai and the Art of Keeping Your Dreams Alive Copy

## Maya Thoresen

# REVIEW

Reviews and feedback help improve this book and the author. If you enjoy this book, we would greatly appreciate it if you could take a few moments to share your opinion and post a review on Amazon. Thank you!

# ABOUT THE AUTHOR

Maya Thoresen is a world traveler and lifestyle coach. In her twenties, she immigrated to the United States and was taken aback by the hectic lifestyle that many Americans practice. Now she works as a writer and mentor, helping people make their lives both simpler and richer. Seeking to combine peace and productivity, Maya has explored philosophies from around the world, from Danish Hygge to the Japanese discipline of Ikigai. Maya endeavors to reach people who are caught up in the hustle of modern life and help them remember how to enjoy the simpler moments.

## Also by Maya Thoresen

https://www.amazon.com/dp/1720484597

https://www.amazon.com/dp/1671190831

https://www.amazon.com/dp/1983239062

# CONTENTS

# ABOUT THE AUTHOR

Maya Thoresen is a world traveler and lifestyle coach. In her twenties, she immigrated to the United States and was taken aback by the hectic lifestyle that many Americans practice. Now she works as a writer and mentor, helping people make their lives both simpler and richer. Seeking to combine peace and productivity, Maya has explored philosophies from around the world, from Danish Hygge to the Japanese discipline of Ikigai. Maya endeavors to reach people who are caught up in the hustle of modern life and help them remember how to enjoy the simpler moments.

### Also by Maya Thoresen

https://www.amazon.com/dp/1720484597

https://www.amazon.com/dp/1671190831

https://www.amazon.com/dp/1983239062

# INTRODUCTION

F irst, there's nothing.

Then there's a noise. It's so annoying. It's growing louder, more insistent.

From your comfortable blur, your senses start to awaken along with your body and mind. Your consciousness kicks in.

You were asleep. That noise is your alarm. It's time to wake up and start your day.

Read those words and think about that scenario. How does it make you feel?

You may be tempted to lie to yourself here. In fact, I can already guess how some of you are answering this question:

*"Mornings? Mornings are great! I just need to have some coffee first... ok, maybe a lot of coffee. But not too much, because then I get all jittery and my stomach gets upset. But once I have coffee, take a shower, brush my teeth, and walk out the door, I feel great.*

*"I look forward to my morning commute because that gives me the time to psych myself up for the day by listening to some music that really pumps me up or calms me down, depending on what's going on. I'm always super-stoked to get going with my daily tasks because my job is totally flexible. I get to work at my own pace and find innovative ways to get things done correctly. Leadership is so collaborative, and we always get rewarded for our hard work and extra hours in ways that are meaningful and help us thrive as human beings.*

*"After work, all of my time is my own to use in ways that satisfy me and enrich my life. I don't have any health concerns because I have access to all the medical care I could possibly need. My mental health has never been better, thanks to the abundant resources available in my community and through my employer.*

*"Overall, I absolutely love waking up in the morning, because I know I'm going to have an awesome day and all of my dreams will come true!"*

This—or some variation of it—is a story I've heard over and over again. But how do I know it's a lie?

To be honest, people who consider themselves *truly happy* know that not every day will be awesome. They understand that all of their dreams will not come true. They accept bad days as an inevitability, and do what they can to honor the bad feelings that come with these experiences. They believe in their ability to survive life's tragedies because above all else, they have a purpose in life.

Maybe you call it your guiding light, or your driving passion. Maybe it's the vision board pinned up above your desk. Maybe you don't even need a name for it, because you feel it deep inside. But the easiest thing to call it is your raison d'etre—a reason for being.

There is no single reason for living. As a matter of fact, most people will have several purposes for living throughout their lifetimes.

Think about your childhood. What do you remember standing out to you as a reason why you were willing to go through all the boring stuff in a day? What did you look forward to every day? For many of us, it was something simple: A favorite television show. A really good meal. Perhaps sports or after-school activities, or spending time with our best friends. Maybe your dreams were bigger—art, riding lessons, maybe summer vacation. Whatever it was, that delight drew you on to explore each new day.

But as we grow older, our outlook changes. During our teenage years, fluctuating hormones, growing bodies, and complicated social relationships often make every choice feel like life or death. From first romance to finding the perfect car, to figuring out what you want to do with the rest of your life before you even graduate from high school, our late teenage and early adult years are chaotic and passionate. It's no wonder many of us lose focus on what we *want* to live for and instead focus on what we think we *should* live for.

For the rest of this book, I'll keep asking you questions about how you are feeling or what you are thinking. But I promise you, you won't be graded on these questions. So, please be honest with yourself. The beauty of working through printed material is that you don't have to respond to these questions out loud (unless you want to, and in that case, go wild!). You may want to write down some of your thoughts. If you feel comfortable keeping a journal, you can jot down your ideas and responses there. Or relax over your questions with a cup of tea—this is your project and yours alone.

With that out of the way, let's go back to the alarm clock. It's blaring in your ear, over and over. You know your comfortable sleepy time is over, and it's time to get on with your day.

How do you *really* feel in this situation?

For many of us, mornings are filled with anxiety, reluctance, and maybe even anger. Many of us flood our systems with caffeine and sugar to not only provide a rush of energy and adrenaline but to also stimulate the endorphins and dopamine that help us ignore our more uncomfortable feelings. With this chemical push to get things done, we're more productive. We clear out our to-do list, earn our living, and even earn some praise. The validation provides even more chemical stimulation, and we feel good about having accomplished so many things and making so many people happy.

That's great. But beyond making your boss happy, why are you getting up in the morning? Is this your reason for living?

Nearly all of us would say yes. We need to work so we can make the money we need to live. Our homes, our food, our transportation, the tools we use to do our jobs—all of these things cost money, so we need to make money in order to stay alive. And with the cost of living rising and bosses demanding perfection on tight deadlines and tighter budgets, our stress levels are rising right along with it.

That's the way we stay alive. But it's not our reason *to* live. You can do a job and do it well without it being your reason for living... as long as you understand what that reason actually is.

That being said, perhaps productivity is your reason for living. But what is it about productivity that you love? Is it the credit and acknowledgment? Having the self-discipline to sacrifice your well-being for the success of your job? Earning big paychecks? Owning a fancy car? Rising to the top? If that's where your heart lies, those are all great things. But if it's not, please consider these questions honestly while you're reading this book.

Ikigai (pronounced "ee-key-GUY") has gained popularity as the "Japanese secret of longevity", but there's more to it than that. We're told that Ikigai is a productivity philosophy from Okinawa, Japan that has led to their longer, happier lives. But that definition isn't entirely correct. Outside of Japan, it's hard to find accurate information on the topic.

In Japanese, Ikigai translates as "the benefit of life", and practitioners consider it a sense of fulfillment that comes from doing what you love. Ikigai encompasses your reason for living, but it doesn't have to be a particularly productive reason. As many experts on the topic have pointed out, Ikigai can be something intangible, like artistic passion or a relationship with a child. It can even mean appreciation for a special routine. Your reason for getting up in the morning may just be because having a cup of coffee while the sun rises makes you feel connected to the planet.

Of course, there's nothing wrong with applying the tenets of Ikigai to your productivity. In fact, this is an area where many of us need assistance finding our focus.

At the same time, we often have something personal that motivates our productivity. As you read this book, I want you to be open and honest with yourself about your reasons for living, and your feelings about why you do what you do. While you look over these exercises, unleash your inner toddler and ask yourself "but why?" until you run out of answers. You might discover a few more details behind your reasons for being.

It's okay to feel a little lost when you first start searching for your Ikigai. Maybe you want to end world hunger. Maybe you want an interlude for peaceful thought every morning. Maybe you really, really want to have the best farm on your favorite video game. Whether it's lofty, everyday, or really personal, every person's Ikigai is worthwhile by definition. Let's take a look at a woman named Barb.

Barb's Story

Barb used to be obsessed with her career, and rightly so. She studied Computer Science at Wellesley when it was a brand new department, and immediately excelled in her field despite backlash towards computers as well as women in a technological field. It wasn't easy for women to get into STEM jobs in the 1980s and 1990s, but she managed to break through the glass ceiling in IT Systems Development.

After a few years, Barb met Dave at a local bar's trivia night. They hit it off, and she put her career on hold to get married and have a family. They divorced—amicably—when the kids were in middle school, but they're still quite cordial. In fact, Dave helped her with the kids so she could go back to school and get her Masters in Information Technology (UMass).

The thing is, when Barb returned to school for her Masters, she rediscovered how very good she is. She was hired by a local up-and-coming business before she even fully had her diploma in hand. With work and determination, her career skyrocketed once more.

Barb's first wake-up call was when she was late to her daughter Rebecca's wedding rehearsal because of a last-minute patch. The team could have handled it, but Barb didn't get to this level in her career by letting other people take care of things.

A few years later, Barb's daughter announced she was expecting. As she sat at the baby shower, Barb realized she didn't recognize anyone there besides her daughter. The guests knew more about Rebecca than she did—what she planned to name her baby, what gender she was hoping for, even how the couple's dogs were taking the changes. Barb didn't know any of these things about her daughter, and that made her feel ashamed of her distance from her children.

Barb decided to step back from her corporate role and take a more relaxed, part-time IT leadership role for a small company in between her home and Rebecca's. This was probably the best time in Barb's life, as she was growing closer to her daughter and granddaughter, and was fully in charge of an IT team. Sure, it was a tiny team of three, but it was her tiny team, and everyone got along famously. Then Covid hit, and while she lost her job, she was very happy to get through the whole thing with her family and her health.

Thankfully, Barb is of an age where she qualifies for retirement payout from her years of corporate hustling. She's received an impressive pension, plus she made some fantastic investments over the years. She doesn't really have a lot of material wants, so what she has is more than adequate. She sold her house for a one-bedroom condo and still drives the Mercedes she bought in 1999.

If Barb had one wish, it would be to have a do-over with her son Timothy. While Barb was able to re-establish a relationship with Rebecca, Timothy is a lot harder. Not only does Tim have a lot of resentment towards Barb for prioritizing her career, but he also lives in Alaska. He works for the National Park Service, and Barb is incredibly proud of him. She wishes she could tell him that, but their relationship has dwindled down to occasional texts and holiday calls. She's just not sure what to do about that.

Overall, Barb thinks she's happy, but the fact is that she's not 100% sure about it, and that makes her wonder sometimes. She's aware that she's spending more time at Becky's house lately and avoiding her own condo, but she is trying to not really think about why or what that might mean. She knows that she's irritated by how cluttered her condo is getting and that she can't seem to get on top of anything. In fact, she constantly feels like she's trying to catch up with something.

Barb knows she has a pretty great life on paper, but she's also had too much time to think about The Should'ves. Her days are pretty regular and busy—she wakes up and heads to Becky's house as everyone is leaving for work. Even on the weekends, the family has breakfast together, or she and her granddaughter meet with Dave at the local coffee shop. It's not that there's anything really bad in her life... she just wants to find a way to enjoy things again.

Clearly, Barb needs to make some changes. Since you're holding this book, you probably feel the same. But I'd like to warn you that any changes you want to make after reading this book will not happen overnight. So don't bite off more than you can chew; Ikigai is all about little nibbles that you can absorb at your own pace. The goal here is not to uproot your life so you can love everything about it, but to figure out how to incorporate your raison d'etre into your everyday routine so that you can enjoy more moments in your life.

Though Ikigai seems to lead to longer lifespans, discovering and honoring your Ikigai does not guarantee a long life. There are plenty of lifestyle choices and involuntary conditions that can impact your life span—anything from diet and exercise to hereditary health situations. Risky behaviors and plain old accidents may impact your longevity (smoking, contact sports, extreme sports, jaywalking, aggressive driving and so on).

The purpose of this book is to connect you more directly with your inner motivation. When discussing Ikigai, many researchers refer to the "flow state." That's that wonderful moment of balance where your skills and the needs of the moment come together, where you're confident, effective, and hardly thinking about the problem at all. Think of a surfer riding the wave—they're making a thousand tiny decisions every minute, but they don't think they're working at all. That moment when an artist is lost in their creation? That's the flow state.

Someone in the flow state may not feel like they're working, but they're being incredibly productive. Experts explain that this is part of the philosophy of Ikigai, but not the entire definition. Ikigai allows individuals to live in a sort of lasting flow, where they can navigate their stresses in a balanced and even enthusiastic manner.

For those who live in the flow state, there is more reason to live than to despair, and these people celebrate finding the moments that honor that desire. Those who have a strong connection with their life have been found to have more meaningful and longer lives.

Many of us struggle with finding meaning in our lives. We may really enjoy our job, our house, our family, and our social lives, but it's possible that none of those are really motivating our lives.

Through a series of exercises, we'll explore what Ikigai is, and ways to practice the concepts of Ikigai. In doing this, I hope you'll come to understand what has meaning to you, and how you can use this information to live a more involved, fuller life with greater appreciation for each day.

If you struggle with mental health issues such as depression or anxiety, you may wish to discuss Ikigai with your medical support team to help you incorporate it correctly in your toolbox.

Please keep in mind that any changes Ikigai creates in your outlook will not be immediate. But being conscious of your Ikigai can help you be present in your own life, regardless of how much of the Ikigai philosophy you can incorporate into your life at this exact moment.

Realizing your Ikigai is an amazing first step in finding a new perspective on life, but each choice you make and action you take will impact your Ikigai. Honoring your Ikigai may not be a linear path. It may change repeatedly over time. However, you can make goals, plans, and dreams based on your Ikigai. You can allow your Ikigai to help you make future decisions.

You have a choice as to how meaningful your life is to you. You can choose your reason for living. You have an opportunity to truly enjoy your life.

Are you ready?

## Exercise One:  What Is The Meaning of Life?

The first part of this exercise is the title.  When you hear the question "what is the meaning of life?", how do you feel?

When faced with this question, many people report feeling:

- Nauseous

- Anxious

- Fearful

- Overwhelmed

- Frustrated

- Sad

There have been many studies done on why we react so negatively to the mere thought of considering our life's meaning.  Why is it so hard for us to think beyond our daily activities?

Many feel that we want our lives to have meaning so that we can feel in control, even though we know logically that we have very little control over most of the situations in our lives.

Some feel that knowing that life has a purpose motivates them through tough times. Feeling that there is a greater good or reward for their struggles can help them see a reason for enduring personal setbacks or tragedies.

In the 1991 film *City Slickers*, the character Curly, played by Jack Palance, defines life as "this," holding up one finger.  Curly provides this wisdom to Billy Crystal's character but passes away before he elaborates on what that means.  The movie follows the main characters through the challenges and triumphs of an old-fashioned cowboy cattle drive, but ultimately, they discover what "this" is—complete with Curly's finger gesture. "This" is different for every person; the secret is sticking with whatever means most to you.

The meaning of life and your reason for living may be entwined, or they may be only loosely connected. However, understanding what the raison d'etre truly means to you can help you step closer to discovering your reason for living.

Right now, what would you say is the meaning of life? What is the first thing that comes to mind when I ask that question?

You don't have to form a full thought or be descriptive. It doesn't have to make sense or be logical.

The first thing that comes to mind might be something that feels "silly," like ice cream, sandal weather, or snuggling with your pet. You might be surprised to learn that these things aren't silly at all!

You might have had the feeling that the question was coming, based on the discussion before it, but were you ready with an answer when the question was finally asked, or did you still find your mind filled with a bunch of different words that felt like mental garbage?

Or did you blank entirely? Did you find that as all of your memories and feelings came rushing through your mind, you couldn't latch onto anything so powerful that you would call it the meaning of life?

This confusion many of you are likely experiencing right now is typical. Many people aren't able to answer that question without significant preparation. Even then, they may doubt their response. For those of you who felt confident with your initial response, how do you feel now that you've read that some people struggle to answer this question?

Are you starting to feel a little bit of panic that you're doing this exercise all wrong?

You're not.

Thinking about the meaning of life is uncomfortable because it reminds us of our own limited time on this planet. It makes us wonder if we matter.

Thinking about these things too deeply has driven many great minds to exploration throughout the years, from philosophers and mathematicians to artists and astronomers. Though it is tempting to explore all their philosophical rabbit trails, we're not going quite that deep. This is not an exercise in harnessing the teachings of every well-known psychologist or analyst, but rather a way to connect to the things that are important to you.

The simpler the answer, the more information you gain about your perspective and priorities. If the first thing that popped into your mind was "ice cream," you might initially worry that "ice cream is the meaning of life" is the most ridiculous thought you've ever had.

But it isn't. What does ice cream represent for you at this moment? Maybe you're hungry. Eating and nourishing your body are important parts of the human experience. Maybe ice cream is tied to your happiest memories. Maybe ice cream is a comfort food, and you're feeling vulnerable, in need of all the soothing things you can gather into your nest. Perhaps you'd like a delicious reward for meeting some kind of goal.

Right now, I want you to hold the first few things that come to mind in your memory, or jot them down if you feel comfortable with that. I don't want you to spend too much time thinking about or analyzing what they might mean just yet.

Instead, I want you to stick with the question, "What is the meaning of life?" You don't need to obsess over it or make it a serious part of your daily meditation if that isn't comfortable for you. I just want you to consider it from time to time. Perhaps you're sitting in the sunlight with your family and friends gathered around you, and the words, "This is the meaning of life" come to you. Maybe you're having a rough day, and as tears swell behind your eyes, you think "is this the meaning of life?"

But again, don't dwell on this, and don't feel the need to go too deep. Let it linger in your mind without taking up too much real estate. We're going to build on this thought as we process new details about Ikigai, which may help you learn a little more about yourself and what the meaning of life is to you.

For now, stop obsessing, and read on.  But as I mentioned before, if something feels important, please feel free to take notes and jot down thoughts—this is all about self-discovery, and sometimes you need to draw a map of your journey as you go along.

Now let's untangle the concept of Ikigai—from the popular "westernized" version, to the more traditional practice of Ikigai among the Japanese.  Then we'll take some time to process what we've discussed with another exercise.

# WHAT IS IKIGAI?

For many people in the Western hemisphere, the word "ikigai" is still a new and mysterious concept.

You may have heard about it from the book *Ikigai: The Japanese Secret to a Long and Happy Life* by Héctor Garcia and Francesc Miralles. This best-selling book has opened the doors to a lifestyle practiced by the citizens of Ogimi Village, Okinawa Prefecture, Japan. This particular village was chosen because it is one of the world's "Blue Zones," in which people have naturally higher lifespans with fewer long-term health complaints. [If you'd like, you can check out https://www.bluezones.com/about/history/ for more information about Blue Zones.] Garcia and Miralles spent time with individuals who have spent their lives in this particular village to learn the secret to aging well and happily.

The term *Ikigai* combines the Japanese words *iki*, meaning "life" or "alive," and *gai*, which means "benefit," or "worth." While these are not exact translations, the overall casual English definition of Ikigai is "a purpose for life" or "a reason to be alive."

But what exactly does that mean? And perhaps more curiously, what does it have to do with a long life?

It turns out that a long life and a passion for living are directly related. Let's take a closer look.

## The Origin of Ikigai

Calling Ikigai the "secret to a long life" is a little misleading. Unfortunately, no magic and no philosophy can guarantee an increase in anyone's lifespan. Illness, accidents, and genetics are all beyond our control at this point in time, though it is possible that technological advances in medicine may make us less fragile than we are today. However, at the core of Ikigai is the belief that having a reason to live can help make every day feel more worthwhile, no matter how many days you live.

We all know our decisions can contribute to a longer life. Women's magazines, newspapers, and Facebook ads all shout it at us a dozen times a day, until we're overwhelmed and flooded by information.

Sure, the choices people make in their diet and eating habits can impact their overall wellness, and Garcia and Miralles outline some of the dietary patterns shared by those who live in Blue Zones. This diet includes fats, oils, sodium, carbs, and sugar—all the alleged "bad" things. However, meals are designed not just to be consumed as fuel but to be enjoyed as an experience. To these individuals, a meal that is pleasurable to the mouth, the body, and the mind is more filling than one that drowns out emotions with physical fullness. Exercise is important, but regular, enjoyable physical movement is better than pushing yourself on the treadmill or the stair-stepper. The Okinawan villagers don't experience a longer lifespan by pushing their bodies to the limits with deprivation dieting and extreme physical training, but through frequently moving in a way that is meaningful and pleasant to them.

Many believe that what ties these physical practices to greater satisfaction in life is the sense of purpose that comes with having an Ikigai—reason to live.

Let's go back to that ice cream from the first exercise. (My apologies if ice cream isn't really your thing—please feel free to replace it with anything that's more relevant to you!)

As mentioned, ice cream often means more than a delicious frozen treat. Let's say you're about to have a really bad day. Maybe you're going to do something you've been putting off because you don't want to do it. Perhaps you know an awkward conversation is on the horizon. Or maybe you're doing something life-changing, like starting a new job, but the anticipation is making you feel emotionally off-kilter.

In this situation, it is not uncommon for many of us to soothe our troubled souls with a treat—like an ice cream. We think of it as bribery in this case, the same way we might sweet-talk to a cranky toddler. "If you do the yucky thing without being bad, you get the good treat!"

Think of Ikigai as a way to normalize bribery and make it seem as though the yucky thing is just a mild inconvenience that lies on the way to your ice cream. "This evening I will have ice cream, and I always enjoy my evening ice cream. Once I get through this yucky thing, I will be that much closer to my ice cream."

Of course, this reframing of a painful, scary, or just plain awkward situation requires a very strong motivator. For most of us, ice cream isn't enough to get us through some of the serious events of our lives, like turning in a resignation notice, the passing of a loved one, or having a conflict with someone important to us.

That's why for many people, Ikigai is deeper than simple concepts like ice cream. This is why it's perfectly normal to feel uncomfortable when casually asked about what you feel is the meaning of life. It takes a lot to truly motivate us to forge our own paths.

Ikigai does not attempt to erase traumatic experiences. It is not a sense of thoughtless happiness. The villagers featured in Garcia and Miralles' book were not cartoon-princess characters who shrugged off the painful experiences of their lives.

Instead, Ikigai presents the possibility that your life may have importance beyond your understanding and beyond your current experience. Acknowledging your reason for living provides a sense of purpose and focus, but it doesn't necessarily define your full life experience.

The government of Japan acknowledges the concept of Ikigai on their official website (https://www.japan.go.jp/kizuna/2022/03/ikigai_japanese_secret_to_a_joyful_lif

e.html), confirming that Japanese senior citizens tend to be active individuals. According to this site, a 2018 national survey revealed that 47.5% of Japanese people over the age of 70 are active in jobs, hobbies, and their community. Decreased mental and physical decline among elderly Japanese who practice Ikigai has led the Japanese government to support employment and social engagement for their senior citizens.

But Ikigai is not only a "life hack" for the elderly. Ikigai is a life-long pursuit, and it can shift as your situation changes. Your commitment to your Ikigai may lead to a greater understanding of yourself and what truly gives you purpose and pleasure, allowing you to more deeply define your Ikigai throughout your life.

It's never too late to consider your own Ikigai, just as it's never too late to process trauma or take up a new skill. Let's dive deeper into the many definitions of Ikigai to get more comfortable with the topic.

## Westernized Vs. Japanese Ikigai

The actual definition of Ikigai has shifted over time. As social norms and cultural traditions have adapted to modern situations, the concept of Ikigai has changed a bit.

Many people consider Mieko Kamimya's *Ikigai ni Tsuite (On the Meaning of Life)* to be the ultimate definition of Ikigai and the concepts associated with it. However, Mieko Kamimya passed away in 1979. Despite being a noted psychiatrist, author, and translator during her lifetime, she is not well known within Japan or internationally, and her work unfortunately remains largely ignored in modern conversations about Ikigai.

Ikigai is frequently defined as a passion that lies at the intersection of what you love, what you're good at, and what other people need. But what that looks like and how you come to that conclusion can vary.

## Western Ikigai

You may have seen a diagram like this before:

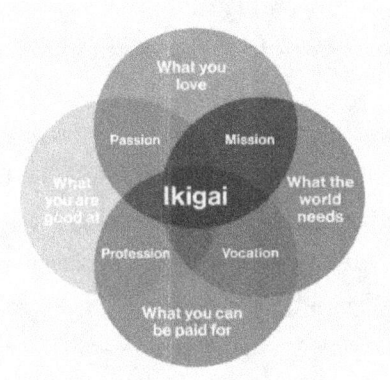

This is a Venn diagram that many people use to demonstrate the essence of Ikigai. However, this diagram is actually attributed to Marc Winn, and it is based on a diagram designed by Spanish author and psychological astrologer Andres Zuzunaga. Though Zuzunaga allegedly created the diagram in 2011, the first public use of the diagram has been noted in Borja Vilaseca's 2012 book *Qué Harías Si No Tuvieras Miedo (What Would You Do If You Weren't Afraid?)*.

Japanologist Nicholas Kemp has shared his discussion with Marc Winn about the Ikigai diagram that has received so much attention in his book *IKIGAI-KAN: Feel a Life Worth Living:*

"The visualization was his own interpretation of the Ikigai concept–and does not originate in Japan or capture the Japanese ethos.

"However, Marc did get it right when stating that Ikigai is a 'reason to get up in the morning' and a 'reason to enjoy life'—and this message has undoubtedly had positive impacts on the many people who have enjoyed his blog post and reflect on his diagram."

On my podcast, Marc kindly explained his creation process:

*"...obviously, I didn't know too much about [Ikigai] other than from that one TED Talk. A lot of people say, why don't you do a book or why don't you do this, why don't you make something of it?, and things like that.*

*"I said, 'Its artistry for me is in that I didn't really think much about it. It was only 45 minutes of my life, and it still grows exponentially, and people write books on it.'"*

But this doesn't mean that this diagram is necessarily wrong—it's just not an accurate reflection of how many Japanese people experience Ikigai. For many, Ikigai can be a relationship with another individual, a ritual that brings peace and balance, or an action that brings a certain result. If a mother were to say her children are her reason for living, for example, she's not getting paid in the traditional sense with money, but with the love of her children and the many moments she cherishes with them.

So should you completely ignore this method of connecting with Ikigai? Of course not! We all have different paths to follow as we learn about ourselves. The diagram presented is actually a pretty neat way to find out more about your passions.

Let's take a look at the diagram in more detail to learn how it works, and how it relates to our possible life's purpose.

## A Purposeful Exercise

Despite its disputed connection to Ikigai, Zuzunaga's Diagram of Purpose isn't without value. In fact, it is a fantastic tool to help many individuals connect to the concept of Ikigai, even if it isn't 100% correct. Let's dig deeper into what each section means.

If you feel comfortable doing so, feel free to make a diagram of your own so you can try it out for yourself. For the time being, just draw three big circles that meet in the middle like the one above.

For each circle, list your answers to one of these questions:

- **What do you love?** This is based purely on your preferences and can include absolutely anything. Ice cream. Dogs. The way the sun shines through the leaves in the trees during your morning commute. The way a person's face changes when they suddenly understand something that has confused them. Money.

Don't be shy in this part of the diagram. Nothing is too minor or silly for you to love. Do you groove on that first whiff of your morning coffee? Get a charge out of neatly organized office supplies? Toss them right in! You're just starting out on this journey, and we always reach for the simplest answers first. Do what it takes to get the creative and introspective juices flowing.

- **What are you good at?** Again, this is based on your experience. Mowing the lawn. Taking notes during lectures or large stressful meetings. Getting the cat to take his evening pill. Making people laugh. Preparing the perfect cup of tea.

- **What does the world need?** Here's where many of us start to put up a mental barricade. What *does* the world need? Depending on your experience and trauma, you may initially stall at this question. Maybe you don't feel like the world needs anything from you in particular.

But push through this fear and discomfort for a second and actually answer the question without modesty.

Let's go back to the ice cream example. It may seem silly, but it isn't at all. In a world in which ice cream is a wonderful treat enjoyed by many, the world needs people to make the ice cream, create the flavors, do the marketing for ice cream brands, sell the ice cream, and so forth.

Perhaps you said you love dogs. The world needs people to adopt dogs, train dogs, groom dogs, and become veterinarians to help dogs stay healthy. The world needs to laugh, learn, and enjoy the beauty of everyday moments.

To round out the examples, let's look at the perfect cup of tea. Many people would feel a lot better if they got to enjoy the perfect cup of tea (or coffee, or ice-cold cola. We don't play favorites here!)

The world needs many things, and even if it doesn't seem like a practical suggestion at this time, this is the space where it's good to jot down potential roles like "ice cream flavor tester" or "dog sitter" or "owner of a tea house" in this circle.

The "world" can also be very small or very big. Your household could be the world, or your world could include the current planet and all future extraterrestrial colonies. It can be both.

- **What can you get paid for doing?** It's important to remember that completing an Ikigai chart is not a legally binding contract. Not even if you do it in permanent marker. Many people hesitate when considering this section of the diagram because they aren't sure they're cut out for whatever role the diagram seems to be leading them toward.

If raking lawns is something you enjoy, and you could potentially get paid a few bucks offering to rake your neighbor's lawn, it belongs on this chart. That's because, while raking leaves for your neighbors certainly isn't a sustainable career path, it could very well be your Ikigai. We'll discuss how some low-paying task like this could be your Ikigai in a moment, but let this be your reminder that nothing is too small, menial, strange, or specific for the purpose of this chart. It's inspiration, not enlistment!

You might be thinking these things aren't a sustainable career, but this exercise isn't necessarily about practicality. You aren't required to be an ice cream taste tester for the rest of your life—this is just a concept that can help you settle your focus and aim your goal.

The places where all three circles meet is considered your purpose—or in the Winn version, your Ikigai. But the other intersections have meaning as well:

- Where *what you love* and *what you are good at* meet is considered your **passion**.

- Where *what you love* and *what the world needs* connect indicates your **mission**.

- The meeting point of *what the world needs* and *what you can get paid for* is your **vocation**.

- *What you are good at* and *what you can get paid for* is your **profession**.

I have to admit, when I first read these descriptions, it sounded like a playground game we used to play, where we would try to tell each other's fortunes with folded paper devices and a little imagination. You might be thinking "So I've been trying to figure out the meaning of life, and the whole time it was where these four circles meet? That's way too simple."

And you're right—it *is* way too simple. And it's also not exactly how many Japanese people experience Ikigai. But it also isn't entirely worth dismissing, even if it is considered a "Westernized" version of Ikigai. Let's take a look at a more traditional version of Ikigai, and then we'll do an exercise to help you discover where you currently are on your path.

## The Japanese Ikigai Experience

Like many intangible concepts and belief systems, the actual experience and attachment to Ikigai vary from person to person.

But many Japanese anthropologists, psychologists, and other experts are stepping forward to note that the Ikigai experiences in Garcia and Miralles' book all come from a sample set of individuals from the same generation and the same village. One community hardly defines any philosophy, culture, or belief system, since that particular community's experience can impact each of these. Think of a culture that experiences floods frequently—their stories and priorities would develop around the realities of rising waters, while those who live in drier climates probably don't have traditions or philosophies that involve an overabundance of water. A desert culture might be built around surviving drought, while a tropical nation might work around monsoons and rainy seasons instead.

Therefore, while the Ikigai thoughts, practices, and methodology shared in the book are true and valid experiences for those who contributed, many have stepped forward to share what they feel is a more "traditional" expression of Ikigai.

This book is not an argument about Western versus Eastern Ikigai—in fact, there are many similarities in each approach. Like each community, each individual is different and will have a different personal philosophy. Therefore, there is no "true" form of Ikigai. The good news is, that makes it impossible for you to "do it the wrong way."

Many people feel limited when exploring a type of philosophy or belief system that is unfamiliar to them. This is understandable, especially in a world where we are all working harder on cultural sensitivity and appreciation instead of appropriation.

When approaching your own expression and connection to Ikigai, bear in mind that attempting to understand and incorporate the concept into your life is generally an appreciative act. You won't be an Ikigai "Master" after reading this book and applying the concepts to your own life, but you will have a clearer understanding of some of the ways in which other cultures structure their philosophy to balance their lives and overall health.

As you're learning about the concept of Ikigai and the ways in which it can express itself, I encourage you to think about which angle might help you connect with your passion and reason for living. We'll continue to work on this connection through the next few exercises, too.

## What Question Are you Trying to Answer?

The concept of Ikigai, in Westernized and the Japanese expression of the term, is truly about finding something to live for. This form of Ikigai strives to answer questions like:

- Why do you wake up in the morning?

- Why do you get out of bed?

- What motivates you to continue going to your job?

- What part of the day do you look forward to the most?

These experts and traditional Ikigai practitioners argue that anyone's reason for living or meaning of life—their Ikigai—doesn't necessarily have to be related to their job, but rather what they do every day.

Rather than asking *"What do I want to do every day?"* this practice of Ikigai asks everyone *"Why do you continue doing what you do every day?"*

In many cases, these are very similar questions. If you love what you do every day, then it's easy to say that you continue because you love it. You have no reason to consider anything else. In this version of Ikigai, however, what you *do* and what you *love to do* can be quite different.

According to award-winning author Ken Mogi, a Japanese neuroscientist who has worked as a researcher at Sony Computer Science Laboratories, "Japanese do not need a grandiose motivational framework to keep going, but rely more on the little rituals in their daily routines."

Many Ikigai practitioners and experts agree that one's Ikigai should not be a massive, potentially unattainable goal. While the intersection of the four circles in the Westernized Venn diagram can absolutely help you discern and describe your marketable talents, you may find that the word that appears in the center of the diagram isn't exactly something you can do easily. In many professions, you must meet a list of educational requirements before you can legally do that job. You may need to obtain state-mandated licenses or certifications before you get started. At the very least, you'll need to find someone who is hiring and complete whatever training is required for a new hire.

And that's assuming that there's actually a market in your area for whatever is at the center of your Ikigai. Discovering that your ultimate dream is to become a teacher for hearing-impaired children can be heartwarming, but also difficult if you live in an extremely rural area with very few children.

I have found that many people have become discouraged by the results they received from completing a Westernized Ikigai diagram, if only because the steps involved in reaching that goal are too tall for the average person to navigate. Going to school can be expensive and time-consuming. We have bills to pay, children to raise, hobbies to pursue, and in many cases, more things to worry about than time to worry about them.

That can feel—or *be*—overwhelming. But what if we take an approach to Ikigai that provides an outlook based on an existing situation or connection?

## More Focus, Less Pressure

The more traditional expression of Ikigai, according to the practitioners and experts, is that of a beloved connection. That could be to a person—a child, a spouse, a dear friend. Your reason to live, to do what you do every day, or why you look forward to each new day, could be because you want to see that person or people live and thrive.

This might also be a connection to a routine. One example that is used frequently to explain this type of Ikigai is that of drinking a cup of coffee every morning, but it could be any routine that you truly enjoy.

Maybe you like to drive a certain way to work or school. You enjoy the familiar landmarks, and any changes along the route are as exciting as a new chapter of a book. Whenever a tree falls, a field is planted, or a house is offered for sale along these roads, you have been there to witness it. While this may not be your entire reason for living, you've come to enjoy this particular journey. You're attached to it. Taking another route is out of the question, and even a perfectly reasonable detour seems like a huge hassle. This is your routine, which you are devoted to because it makes sense and feels familiar.

Now ask yourself if you have any patterns or activities that you're even more devoted to. One that many people report is a bedtime routine. Some sleep experts believe that creating a distinct routine prior to going to bed will help your body become conditioned to the activities, allowing your brain and body to subconsciously wind down when you're ready to go to sleep. Folks have also discovered that they find themselves looking forward to these routines, and getting a little extra burst of joy when they're preparing for sleep. As a result, they have reported overall better and longer sleep.

Some Ikigai practitioners and experts argue that the Western diagram doesn't accommodate for Ikigai changing over time. If your relationship with a person changes, perhaps they fade out of focus as your Ikigai. A new job could bring with it a new daily pattern, just as a new home could change your bedtime routine.

So Ikigai isn't your goal state. Instead, it's a flowing practice of finding bliss in everyday pleasures. Sure, the focus of this bliss can be very specific, but it's also possible to have multiple reasons for living. The reasons why you look forward to each day in your life may change over time.

These practitioners believe that, as humans, we can—and often do—change throughout our lives. Why should we be held back by a previously-held Ikigai, rather than growing into a new situation with a new Ikigai?

Some hypothesize that an Ikigai might be a life-long commitment for the Okinawan villagers due to their lifestyle. Living on an island provides opportunities, but can limit them as well. Many among today's younger generations enjoy a lifestyle where they can travel wherever they want at any time. They have access to education in nearly any topic you can imagine. The internet has allowed experts in any topic the opportunity to share their insights. You can virtually work in a country where you've never set foot.

Differences in lifestyle may be the reason behind the differences in the expression of Ikigai. Someone who has lived 100 years or longer in the same place will likely have a different outlook on their goals and general lifestyle than someone who has grown up moving from city to city, or who has worked on a contractual job basis, going from site to site.

If your life is a steady and predictable stream with few changes, you may feel more empowered to make a lifelong goal and stick to it forever. After all, you have little to risk, and sharp focus, discipline, and dedication are common ingredients in so-called "Recipes for Success."

On the other hand, if your life has been centered around change and adaptability, you probably feel like making a forever-long commitment to anything is a huge risk. If every day is a new schedule, a new routine, and a new set of faces, it doesn't make sense to dedicate yourself to anything that requires stability—you'd just be setting yourself up for failure.

Therefore, many writers pause their discussion of Ikigai here. Neither definition or expression is "right" or "wrong." In fact, the true definition of Ikigai for you will be highly individual. If it suits you better to sharpen your laser focus on a lifelong pursuit or ambition, Westernized Ikigai is an excellent opportunity for you to set the groundwork and boundaries for that opportunity in a logical and safe way. But if you are more interested in figuring out how to focus on your life's purpose amidst all the noise in life, perhaps the traditional expression is a better fit for you.

In our next exercise, we'll apply what we've discussed about Ikigai so far to help you decide which concepts you connect with most, and where you might be struggling to get on board with the overall idea. This should help clarify the idea for you, and help you to relate to some of the concepts we're going to discuss in the next chapter.

## Exercise Two: What Does This Mean to You?

Based on the information we've covered so far, it's time to discover where you connect with the concept of Ikigai, and what it means to you.

It's ok to be pretty confused at this point—in fact, we've barely even scratched the surface of what Ikigai is and how it can relate to all aspects of your life. Don't worry, we'll get into that in the next chapter.

For now, here's something that might help you connect with Ikigai as we've discussed it so far.

First, let's try a little quiz. Answer each of the following questions honestly. I've included some multiple-choice answers to help you sort out your feelings, but your answer doesn't have to fit neatly into these choices. You might have a "yes, but..." or "not really, but kind of..." response, and that's perfectly fine. If you feel comfortable jotting those thoughts in your journal, you might want to reflect on them later. These types of answers can help you really concentrate on your true feelings—what you like, what you don't, what really motivates you. But for now, just focus on answering these questions:

1. When you think of "the future," what do you think of?

   a. A span of time 5-10 years from now.

   b. Old age.

   c. When I start needing help doing things.

   d. I don't really think about the future.

2. How easily can you list 5 reasons why you're happy to be where you are, right now?

   a. I could probably list more than 5.

   b. I'm not sure I could list 5.

c. I can list some things, but I'm not fully confident in my answer.

d. I wouldn't find it very easy.

3. Which of these sets of words are most relatable to you?

a. Goal-oriented, frustrated, future-planning, calmly focused, hyper-vigilant.

b. Overextended, grateful, confused, guilty, content.

c. Overstimulated, unsure, exhausted, giddy, excessive.

d. Underwhelmed, frantic, apathetic, perfectionist, numb.

4. Of the following options, which sounds the most appealing to you?

a. A warm, cozy family-style meal with all of the people you love the most, in which everyone has contributed something to help everyone have a wonderful time.

b. No plans, just peace of mind that nothing terrible has happened, and that I can go to bed knowing I've done the best I could with the resources available to me.

c. A day in which all of my needs are met without question or turmoil, I receive the validation I need, and I find a few reasons to smile here and there.

d. A comfortable space for my body, while my mind can be occupied by only pleasant thoughts, I hear only good music, and there's nothing to worry about.

How did you answer these questions? Were your answers mostly the same letter, or a different letter for each question? Or did you feel like the multiple-choice answers were way off base, and you came up with your own or modified the responses for each question?

There's no tally system here. None of these letters correspond to a number that you can add up to tell you exactly how you should proceed in your Ikigai journey. Instead, I'd like you to take a look at how all of the pieces you've chosen in your responses fit together:

- What do your responses say about your current state of mind? Do you feel this is accurate? Furthermore, is this a state of mind that you would like to maintain, or do you feel that a change is in order?

- What do your answers tell you about how much you value the future? Are you the type of person who carefully and cautiously monitors their career, financial status, and bucket list to make sure you get everything you want out of life, or are you just trying to make it through the days one responsibility at a time?

- What makes you smile? What do you enjoy? What feeling neutralizes all of the bad stuff in life?

You might be looking at your answers and thinking, "That's a lot of questions that I don't think I answered, and what does any of that have to do with Ikigai?"

The first step to finding the meaning of life is being fully engaged in the life you're leading now. Pursuing Ikigai would mean you enjoy being alive and are actively satisfied with your life and prospective future, overall. Folks who feel like this often feel comfortable making more rigid future plans because they can feel confident in their ability to strive for their dreams. Failure isn't a risk for these individuals, because any step forward is a step in the right direction, and a step backward is an important lesson to learn.

But for some of us, our days are a little different. Some days we're sad and don't really feel like engaging with others. Other days we just feel numb and blah, and even spending time with our loved ones doesn't bring us much joy. From one day to the next, you might be angry and irritated, or absolutely beside yourself with delight.

Or maybe you picked up this book because you have never considered your purpose in life. How does that make you feel? Are you a little anxious now because you are just now at a point where you are thinking about the meaning of life? Are you relieved to hear that hardly anyone consciously and deliberately thinks about the meaning of life? If so, you are like many people. The modern world is very busy, and there are distractions everywhere, no matter how hard you try to shut down the outside world.

Everyone is on a different path towards discovering and connecting with their Ikigai. I don't want you to feel pressured yet to create your own diagram or start listing things that you might consider your Ikigai—in fact, I don't want you to feel pressured at all! Instead, I want you to answer two final questions for this exercise, and you might need a few moments to really think about your answers:

- Am I trying to find the meaning of life, or am I trying to find my value?

- Do I want to establish a goal, or am I interested in uncovering everyday bliss?

For most of us, the answer to these questions is a little bit of both. Take your time considering how much each perspective resonates with you. Ultimately, your Ikigai will lead to all of this, but your journey will be different depending on where you start.

# Ikigai and Your Own Life

You may be struggling to connect the "long life" part of Ikigai with having a reason for living. Sure, there's the part where enjoying your life and connecting with it can make you enjoy every moment, but how can that actually make your life longer?

As you may have guessed—or possibly feared—there's more to it than that. While it would be great to follow a process in which all you had to do to live a long and happy life was to understand what you're living for, philosophies and beliefs are rarely so cut and dried.

It's generally agreed among all kinds of scientists, researchers, and medical practitioners that there is no one "secret" to having a long life. In fact, despite our best efforts, we often have little control over our own lifespan.

However, it's equally accepted that our mental health, our emotional health, and our physical health are closely intertwined. When we experience discomfort in one area, the other two are also thrown out of balance. Many experts feel that the best way to achieve health is to work to heal and grow in our minds, our emotional expressions, and our bodies.

Let's start by taking a look at what many experts feel is an ideal recipe for good health, and then think about what can happen when we incorporate Ikigai. You might be surprised at how having a reason to live can enhance your mental health, your emotional health, and your physical health simultaneously.

## Modern Ideas for Living a Long Life

I know that trying to keep up with the modern fads and recommendations about living a long life can be exhausting. One day we're being told that we should do our best to eat as little fat as possible, the next day we're being told that "good" fats like olive oil and avocado will keep us healthier so we can enjoy long, happy lives. All of these studies include credible scientific data, so it's hard to argue with them.

But we've also discovered that human bodies are almost as varied and extraordinary as human minds. No two of them seem to do all of the same things in the same way under the same circumstances. The medication that works very well on a mother can cause an allergic reaction in her biological daughter. A man and his adopted son may have the same rare genetic condition, despite not being related. Medical science has had to find many different ways to treat individuals, rather than using an umbrella treatment for most health situations.

That being said, most health professionals would feel comfortable saying that there are a few general guidelines that can help support your body, such as:

- Get plenty of rest and sleep

- Participate in an amount of physical activity that is realistic for your body

- Drink enough water for your body's needs and activity level

- Follow a diet that is higher in nutritionally dense food than high-sugar or high-fat foods

- Avoid habits like smoking, drinking, or drug use, which can harm your internal organs

As research into biology and medicine continues, we're learning that there's no perfect nor no lab-tested formula that will guarantee perfect health for every individual. If you are concerned about getting the right kind of rest, activity, and nutrition, you may wish to consult with a doctor or medical specialist to help you identify your individual needs and develop a plan for you to follow.

And there's another aspect to our health that can derail even the best-laid health plans: stress. Many health and wellness practitioners would encourage you to "avoid stress" as well. That sounds good when we're finishing our checkup or reading a wellness article over our morning coffee. Right up until the rain starts pouring, the car won't start, or the kid tells you about the science project that's due this morning. All it takes sometimes is a moment of frustration or an accident in the works—something as simple as getting your sleeve caught on the doorknob or tripping over your own feet—to start the heart pumping and the brain racing.

## Stress

Much of what we do during our waking hours is stressful. Our days are filled with subtle pressures and micro-stressors.

Even a simple, regular task can go wrong and set the tone for the rest of the day. What if you were to stumble and spill some of your favorite drink? Will spilling your coffee ruin your entire life? Probably not, but it will set you on edge and inconvenience you. You might have to deal with wet, stained clothing, maybe even burns if the hot liquid hits your skin. All of this will throw your body into a danger response. You might yelp, curse, or find yourself feeling much angrier than you expected. And even though we're typically able to clean up a mess and find a reasonable work-around for anything that got damaged in the spill, it's hard to have a good day after that.

While we can't avoid stress altogether, many experts recommend we find our own ways to mitigate it. You've likely heard of tools like recognizing your boundaries, setting expectations, taking breaks, and using relaxation techniques to find your flow state, where you can avoid worry and simply get into a state of being and doing.

What have you tried to help you cope with stress? Or perhaps I should ask, what has worked, and what hasn't worked so well? Believe it or not, many individuals struggle with using commonly recommended stress reduction tools. Squeezing a ball, tapping, holding ice cubes, and doing controlled breath exercises works for a lot of people, but not for everybody.

Oftentimes, our brains and bodies are doing a little self-sabotage when we're stressed out. The "fight, flight, or freeze" reaction many of us are familiar with can occur in big doses or smaller ones. Whether we're actually paralyzed with fear, or having trouble getting our mouths to synchronize with what we want to say, stress can prevent our brains and our bodies from reaching balance. Our brains kick into an instinct-driven state as our hearts pump adrenaline through the body.

Deep breathing and other relaxation exercises can help you get your body under control. But it takes time and practice, and even then it takes a while to mentally and emotionally recover from this state. Even when you feel better, you might still think about your stress for the rest of the day, or even much longer.

This is where the emotions often chime in. "Why are you still upset? That problem's over! Just get past it!" Whether you're saying these things to yourself or some well-meaning person is saying them to you, they'll still make you feel even worse about your situation. You may feel guilt or anger at yourself, or sadness that you got in that situation in the first place. If you reacted poorly out of instinct, you might be regretful or angry about your choices.

Then the cycle repeats. You are consciously attempting to avoid that situation again while subconsciously working through your emotions. Eventually, and with some effort, many of us are able to process trauma; however, nearly all of us have some kind of background stress. Like the music in a grocery store, this stress is hardly noticeable until it somehow disrupts what you're trying to accomplish.

So what does this all have to do with Ikigai or living for a long time?

If we live in a state where we're constantly stressed and subsequently punishing ourselves emotionally for feeling stress, we're really just sabotaging all three levels of health. We're in mental turmoil from all of the conflicting thoughts, our rapidly-fluctuating emotions have us feeling out of control, and we frequently experience headaches or gastro-intestinal discomfort. Even our immune systems respond poorly to stress.

Ikigai answers the question of *"But what if I didn't have to stress myself about every little thing?"* In times of high tension, what if you could focus on your purpose in life–your reason for living—and march through this unfortunate situation?

Many of us experience stress because we don't know how to let go of the things that stress us. Assuming there was no actual injury, we have a really hard time handling mistakes, embarrassments, and minor failures. Many of us view a simple mistake or accident as a sign of personal failure. You may punish yourself with phrases like "I should have been paying attention!" or "That was all my fault!"

But we could avoid all of the big trauma associated with a little accident if we could abandon that type of mindset all together.

Practicing Ikigai doesn't erase all mistakes or let you shrug off embarrassment. Instead, your constant practice of Ikigai can help you feel more balanced and stable in all areas, so that an event like this doesn't cause suffering—it's just a wobble in the healthy balance of life.

## Finding a Healthy Balance

As we've discussed, many health experts agree that overall health is achieved through the balance of mental, emotional, and physical health. Those who lead a healthy lifestyle generally experience fewer chronic health conditions or serious concerns.

Experts in philosophical and psychological fields may disagree on a lot of things—from where thoughts come from to why we exist—but they will agree that believing you have a purpose for being on this planet can help improve your overall outlook. While our life experiences can impact whether we're more optimistic or pessimistic, our willingness to engage with our own well-being and strive for good health and long life can be related to how much we actually want to live.

Many experts further agree that the mind and emotions can be exercised, just like the body. We can train ourselves to adjust our outlook or reactions to help us experience less stress.

Think of connecting with your Ikigai as a sort of exercise for your mind and your emotions. Understanding your reason for living is the warm-up, but living your life with your Ikigai as your primary focus is a daily workout.

The mere act of identifying your reason for living isn't a magic potion or pill. You don't decide on what the meaning of life is for yourself and then suddenly have no stress and live forever.

Instead, Ikigai is a practice. Like exercise equipment at the gym, deep breathing techniques, and finding physical and mental outlet for your stress, your Ikigai can be considered a tool that must be used in order to help. Just as a hammer can't help you repair anything when it's locked in a box in the garage, your Ikigai cannot help you reach a pleasant state of healthful balance unless it is within easy reach.

Balancing all three aspects of health and wellness—mental, emotional, and physical—can require more energy and resources than some of us have at any given time. It's hard to make time for the gym when you're struggling with an hour-long commute, and you can't spare much time for contemplation when the boss has just popped another spreadsheet onto your monitor. Practicing these concepts is great, but it isn't going to "fix" anything in anyone's life right away.

However, incorporating your Ikigai with your daily life might be a little easier than you think. This is not an "all or nothing" endeavor—you can experience your Ikigai your way, on your terms.

For many of us, our health, our emotions, our motivation, and our general outlook on life are closely linked. But you can find a way to not only honor this connection, but transcend it to find a more peaceful state. Let's look a little closer at the connection between Ikigai, health, and the flow state.

## The Benefit of the Flow State

One of the benefits of practicing a connection to Ikigai is the ease of reaching your "flow state"—the state where you experience minimal bad stress and just enough good stress to help you enjoy the moment. While it's not a magic wand to chase away your stress forever, being able to access and maintain a flow state can help you appreciate your baseline emotional state. With practice, you can recognize when something has changed, empower yourself to explore these complications, and create the tools you need to navigate to a new flow state.

It's important to remember that Ikigai is not a system of beliefs or a full philosophy. It is a concept that can be added to your current beliefs and values, but doesn't necessarily need to define them. Think of it as a lens that you can look through for a clearer view of any situation. As we explored earlier, your Ikigai might express itself as a professional goal, a routine, or any meaningful connection. In fact, it is the connection that seems to be the biggest ingredient in the recipe that turns Ikigai into a calm, peaceful flow state.

The term "flow state" can have different meanings, depending on the source. Philosophically, it is often considered a state of mind in which you are able to consistently create, debate, or converse on a topic at length without pause. Psychologically, some experts believe this is a sort of equilibrium in stress, in which one's emotional state, mental processing, and physical health are in balance. Medically, the flow state is the place where your physical systems—muscles, connective tissue, brain chemicals, hormones, and pain receptors—are all at peak performance, such as you might find in a professional athlete.

Ultimately, most people consider a flow state one in which they aren't struggling in any way. They can focus on what they want to focus on, they can perform the activities they want to do with clarity, and they feel emotionally at ease.

Just as there isn't one single definition for a flow state, there is no strict step-by-step map to help us get there. Whether you're just trying to quiet your mind so you can focus on getting a work task done all at once, or you're training for a marathon, finding a flow state can be a different process from day to day. After all, how often are our days *exactly* the same?

It's this lack of a constant in our lives that often throws our health out of balance. Without a focal point for our lives, we look for comfort and meaning wherever we can find it, and that can be anywhere from controlled substances to a tray of cupcakes. We may take up habits that are physically unhealthy or emotionally damaging. Mental illness, addiction, or emotional upsets may cloud our judgment and leave us feeling vulnerable, yet unable to change our situation.

From a tumultuous state like this, it's almost impossible to find your balance. You may feel literally "at sea", but knowing your own Ikigai can provide you with an anchor.

Many professionals recommend that those who wish to make a significant life change do so in a way that aligns with their current motivation level.

Celebrating your Ikigai can help you find that focus within your life. By connecting with your reason for living, you'll be able to pinpoint motivation that lies beyond the here and now, and with the overall satisfaction level of your life.

Many athletes, performers, artists, and even emergency rescue workers and surgeons have described getting to this flow state as something of a meditative act, in which the mind and body relax beyond any emotional connection to the activity at hand. They transcend the noise in their ears and their thoughts alike. They are able to engage the conscious and subconscious so smoothly that they can perform their craft without a hitch.

Ikigai can provide this focus—a soft mental gaze inward, a focus on something truly cherished deep within. It is, of course, possible to break this focus. Having this focus does not require motivation or determine success. However, this focus—this reason for living or the meaning for your life—can provide a place for your conscious and subconscious mind to rest as you ease into this flow state, even during times of stress.

### Barb's Story

Barb doesn't much like self-reflection. She's always been focused and goal-driven. But when she asks herself questions like "what are you getting up for?" she doesn't know the answer.

That never stopped her before. She won't let it stop her now. So she creates a little structure in her haphazard retirement schedule. She sets her alarm every morning, brews herself a pot of coffee, and writes in her journal for half an hour.

It's not much of a journal—a spiral-bound notebook she picked up at the drug-store—and the entries aren't exactly earthshaking. Not to start with, a just-the-facts recap of the previous day's events. But then the weather creeps in, and then so does Barb's opinion of the weather. One morning, she writes about how the rain reminds her of quiet mornings studying at UMass, and she catches herself smiling.

That smile stays with her all day.

## The Role of Ikigai in Health, Wellness, and Thriving

As mentioned, the link between Ikigai and longevity is not a simple one. Don't think of it as a magic pill, but rather a powerful tool you can use to strengthen the framework of your mental, emotional, and physical well-being. That tool can look different for every practitioner. Maybe you need a gentle guide to help you make subtle changes. Or maybe you're looking for a hammer to drive you toward your goals.

As you'd expect from such a powerful tool, Ikigai looks different for different people. Again, since there are differing views on Ikigai and how to conceptualize your connection with your meaning for living, the exact connection can differ between individuals. So while you're reading, consider the material from the perspective of how *you* relate to the idea of Ikigai and not from a specifically "Westernized" or "Japanese" point of view.

Given the connection we've discussed between mental, emotional, and physical health, it's clear that all three are inextricably intertwined. A sense of purpose or peace can help balance all three, and connecting with your Ikigai might be a good focus to help you maintain that balance. But simply discovering your Ikigai might be just as important to your overall wellness.

In his book *Awakening Your Ikigai: How the Japanese Wake Up to Joy and Purpose Every Day*, Ken Mogi describes the five pillars of Ikigai. According to him, the five pillars—or objectives—of Ikigai include:

- *Pillar 1: Starting small → Focusing on the details.*

- *Pillar 2: Releasing yourself → Accepting who you are.*

- *Pillar 3: Harmony and sustainability → Relying on others.*

- *Pillar 4: The joy of little things → Appreciating sensory pleasure.*

- *Pillar 5: Being in the here and now → Finding your flow.*

Thanks to Mogi's book, these concepts are some of the best-known tenets of Japanese Ikigai. Let's break the pillars down into a bit more detail so you can see how they work in the overall Ikigai practice.

## Mogi's Five Pillars of Ikigai in Detail

At first glance, these five pillars may seem pretty self-explanatory. The words make sense, and they aren't too different from some of the sayings we encounter every day in self-help, therapy, and lifestyle forums.

But, like any adjustment in perspective, understanding the words and incorporating the concept into your lifestyle aren't the same. Ken Mogi provides greater details in his book, of course, but here are some more details about the concepts he describes:

### Pillar 1: Starting Small
You might be thinking, "Focus on details. Sure, I can do that. Let's just look at things more closely going forward."

The process is a little more involved than that. In Mogi's book, he likens the concept of focusing on the details to that of *Kodawari*—the pursuit of perfection.

In a world in which many of us actively struggle to maintain boundaries and avoid a people-pleasing mentality, the word "perfection" has sadly evolved to mean "you'll never be good enough."

But Kodawari has nothing to do with gaining the approval of others. Instead, it is a deep-rooted pride that guides and encourages your attention to detail. It is a self-defined, self-guided level of personal satisfaction with the knowledge that actual perfection cannot be attained. It is not the feeling of "This project will never turn out the way I envision," but rather an attitude of "I am excited to continue working on this project to see how I can continuously improve it and what I can learn. What I do now gives me the opportunity to explore new challenges tomorrow."

Kodawari allows us to pursue perfection in the knowledge that we can, and will, fall short. Small steps toward your goal can give you a feeling of focus and control. No one can attain pure perfection, but we can find joy in the attempt.

## Pillar 2: Releasing Yourself

It interests me that Mogi uses the phrases "release" and "accept" to describe this stage. Many people use similar words when processing trauma or working through self-esteem and confidence issues.

The word "release" indicates letting go of something. We let go of something when it is no longer beneficial to hold onto it—but often, we struggle with letting go. Similarly, the word "accept" also suggests the end of a struggle. Acceptance occurs when we stop fighting the truth.

Many people who have experienced troubles in their mental, emotional, and physical health have difficulty accepting their situation. After all, many cultures value stoicism—the act of pretending we aren't suffering when we are, in fact, in dire need of assistance. Like a child insisting "I'll do it myself!", we may have even actively refused help when we know we desperately need it.

Furthermore, we live in a world in which we know we will not meet the standards of everyone we meet—yet that perfection is still expected. As with the concept of Kodawari, releasing yourself and accepting yourself involve the acceptance that you are not perfect. That you will never be perfect, but each day lets you live a life that truly honors who you are as a person.

## Pillar 3: Harmony and Sustainability

Interestingly enough, the idea of community is important in both Garcia's and Mogi's depictions of Ikigai.

In fact, the concept of a group of people selflessly sustaining each other has been linked to a longer, happier life in many cultures and communities throughout history. Ogimi, Okinawa, Japan. Hunza Valley, Pakistan. Campodimele and Molochio, Italy. All of these villages have been noted for their higher-than-average lifespans, yet they also share another common thread: scarcity.

Even when food or other resources are low, some communities still thrive. Almost every time, those communities are the ones that work together to ensure everyone has the best chance for survival. They pool resources, they provide companionship and comfort to each other, and they meet regularly to foster a sense of solidarity. In essence, connection and acceptance in the community as a whole can amplify your reason for living, your Ikigai.

## Pillar 4: The Joy of Little Things

This is another largely accepted tenet within the various forms of Ikigai. In fact, many philosophies, religious or secular, encourage people to truly take the time to enjoy anything that can be enjoyable.

Maybe you've followed along with the whole "unplugging" trend, or you heard about the "low-dopamine morning" concept that hit the internet in 2023. This involved removing yourself from the phone or other devices, skipping caffeine or heavy exercise, and creating a morning routine rich in relaxation, meditation, and gratitude. Choosing a morning ritual that focuses on peace and serenity gives you something to look forward to and can help set the mood for your day.

The concept of having something to look forward to ties into Mogi's idea of "the joy of little things". He argues that it's not only okay to experience sensory pleasure, but to actively engage our senses to find more pleasure in the simplest of experiences. To use our examples from earlier, this could include using our five senses to discover:

- Why is ice cream so enjoyable?

- What feelings do you get when you play with dogs?

- What makes this the perfect cup of tea?

Our negative feelings are valid, but sometimes they can overshadow or invalidate our more positive emotions. Rather than allowing ourselves to dwell on the hardships of the day, what if we were to allow ourselves to take in the joy of all the small things that went well?

### Pillar 5: Being in the Here and Now

Kodawari—the commitment to perfection—blends with the flow state to help you stay in the moment. Western philosophers and psychologists may refer to this as connecting with your inner child. Generally speaking, children have a deeper connection to the present moment than they do to the past, and their conception of the future means very little to them. The present is their reality, so all of their actions and decisions are based on the here and now.

As we grow older, we learn more about consequences and become more cautious in our approach to the world. We don't want anything bad to happen. We don't want to hurt anyone's feelings. We don't want to feel awkward or ashamed of ourselves.

Being in the here and now doesn't require us to pursue our every impulse or gobble our food—even if it's ice cream—but it does ask us to consider what we would do from moment to moment if we didn't limit ourselves. Many of us restrict our actions, conversations, and even our emotional expressions so that we only do what we're supposed to do. It's natural to consider the people who are important to you, but many of us have shaped ourselves to suit our parents, our bosses, even our friends. Throughout our lives, we have learned the hard way to meet the expectations of others.

Being in the here and now, however, asks you to honor everyone's boundaries and wishes—especially your own.

These five pillars are, again, just one method to celebrate and express Ikigai. Ken Mogi's concepts reflect principles in both Westernized and a more traditional understanding of Ikigai, but you may find that your journey towards Ikigai and wellness takes a bit of a different path.

Your path won't be like everybody else's. So how do you line up these pillars to apply to your own life?

You can find dozens of ways to tie all of these concepts together. Akihiro Hasegawa, one of Japan's leading Ikigai researchers, has created a chart that demonstrates what he calls "the Constituent Elements of Ikigai." He has studied the work of Mieko Kamiya and explains that Ikigai can be considered from two different approaches:

- People have an object of Ikigai

- People have a feeling (Ikigai-kan) inspired by their object of Ikigai

Surprisingly, Hasegawa's interest in Ikigai is largely academic, inspired by his work as a clinical psychologist at a hospital for dementia patients. As he worked, Hasegawa noticed that the cognitive decline process was remarkably slower in patients who reported having Ikigai, compared to those who did not seem to feel any strong reason for living.

In his research, Hasegawa uses this chart to demonstrate how the different expressions of Ikigai are combined within the Self:

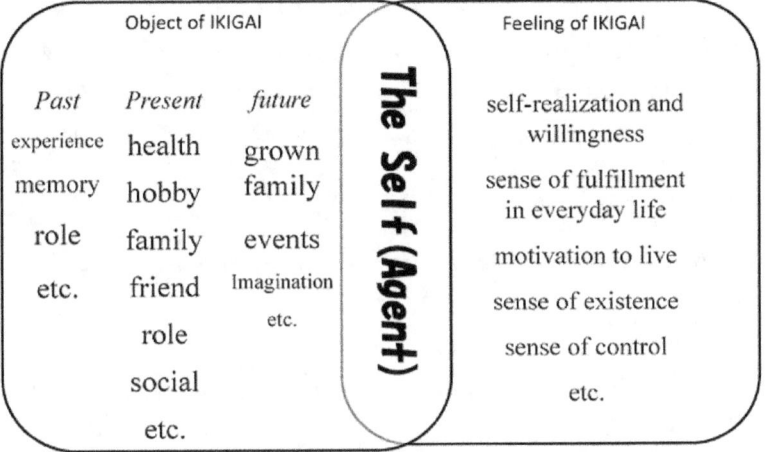

Fig. 1 : Constituent elements of "Ikigai" (Hasegawa, etal., 2001)
"Ikigai" can be defined as "a sense of being alive now, an individual's consciousness as a motive to live.".
"IKIGAI" is work of the mind which integrated an "object of IKIGAI" and "Feeling of IKIGAI".

The Self in this case is our conscious being—the thoughts, logic, and values we use to make our decisions. The Self is who you understand yourself to be and the agent of everything you do.

Understanding these elements will help you consciously connect with your reason for living. Working from everything you know, everything you do, everything you hope for, and everything you are, you can find that peak where your reason for living exists. This, according to Hasegawa, is the expression of Ikigai.

In discussions of Ikigai, Hasegawa has described it as a sense of being alive in the present moment, blended with individual self-awareness and an open curiosity about what could happen next. This combination provides people with a sense of meaning that propels them through their daily lives.

In his 1998 letter to the British Geriatrics Society, researcher Noriyuki Nakanishi, a Department of Public Health researcher at Osaka University Medical School, describes "'Ikigai' in older Japanese people" this way:

*"The word 'ikigai' is usually used to indicate the source of value in one's life or the things that make one's life worthwhile (for example, one might say: "This child is my ikigai"). Secondly, the word is used to refer to mental and spiritual circumstances under which individuals feel that their lives are valuable. There is a difference between ikigai and the sense of well-being. Ikigai is more concerned with the future: for example, even when one feels that one's present life is dark, possessing a desire or goal for the future allows one to feel ikigai.*

*"Ikigai gives individuals a sense of a life worth living. It is not necessarily related to economic status.*

*"Ikigai is personal; it reflects the inner self of an individual and expresses that faithfully.*

*"It establishes a unique mental world in which the individual can feel at ease."*

There is no single path to connect each human with their Ikigai. Instead, finding your Ikigai is much like finding your morals, values, and spirituality. However, various experts who practice, study, and incorporate Ikigai into their scientific research have shared their insight into the process. They agree that there can be different ways in which people can experience Ikigai. Self-reflection is key, so you need to tune in to your own heart and mind to follow your own path toward your Ikigai.

Many practitioners feel that Ikigai shouldn't be a rigid and impossible goal, but rather a fluid, changeable passion that requires finesse and attention. Ken Mogi's Five Pillars of Ikigai and Akihiro Hasegawa's Constituent Elements of Ikigai are similar, in that they require inward reflection and the disregard for exterior influences like money or pleasing others. But maybe you resonate with the Marc Winn diagram, feeling led to find Ikigai at the meeting place of what you love to do, what you're good at, what the world needs, and what you can get paid to do.

Ultimately, the practice of Ikigai is just that—*practice*. Discovering your reason to live is a commitment. Many of us are wary of long-term loyalty—either because we've never personally experienced it, or because our trauma has taught us that no bond is unbreakable. It doesn't matter *how* you find your Ikigai, only *that* you do.

The goal of Ikigai is to bring greater peace to your life, not more stress.  Sometimes we might be more prepared for lighter doses of major life changes, while at other times, we need to take a giant leap outside of our comfort zone in order to enact change.  Other times, we're not exactly sure what we're expecting or what we actually want to change.  Our next exercise will help with that dilemma.

You likely picked up this book because the title or description spoke to you.  You may feel strongly connected to your reason for living, and you're only reading this to see if there are any ways you can connect more intentionally with what you feel is the meaning of life.  On the other hand, you might have never considered your reason for living before picking up this book.

At any moment in our lives, we are all on a different journey.  This exercise will help you figure out where you are at this moment, where you would like to go, and how quickly you'd like to get there.

## Exercise Three: Spot the Differences - Your Life Now Versus Finding Your Ikigai

Most people don't make major changes in our lives without having a very good reason.  In fact, a surprising number of us stubbornly refuse to budge from even the smallest inconvenience.

We all have different priorities, and we all have our own motivations for the ways in which we structure our lives.

Sound familiar?

Many people already practice Ikigai on an instinctive level, creating a strong attachment to a behavior, routine, object, or goal in their lives.  However, these current attachments may not be very healthy. A workaholic may focus on their career and neglect recreation, relationships, and even their health. Someone suffering from substance addiction may feel that feeding the addiction is the reason to live. But on a deeper level, they know this isn't, or at least shouldn't be, true.

Not all habits are full-blown addictions, but our unwillingness to let go of old behavior can be stronger than we expect.

When you connect with your Ikigai, you are committing to a certain level of focus and release. You are not forcing control upon your Ikigai. You are not developing a dependency on your Ikigai. You are not making your Ikigai an obsession or a scapegoat for your choices.

Instead, you're simply changing your focus on whatever it is that guides your life.

And that change can be closer than you think. If you decided in the last exercise that finding your Ikigai looks like a worthwhile goal, then you are allowing this goal to help guide you in your decisions. Your actions, your mindset, and your reality are coordinated to help you reach this goal. Regardless of how much closer you got to your goal today, tomorrow is another day to try again.

If you have decided that a flexible, multi-faceted, Ikigai experience would help you engage more with a reason for living, you are allowing your dedication to your Ikigai to guide your focus.

The important question is: are you doing these exercises because you want to, or because you feel like you should?

It's okay to answer honestly. You cannot change any behaviors you don't actually want to change.

Which brings us right back to Ikigai. You won't truly connect with your Ikigai if it's something you don't truly feel is worth living for.

Don't feel rushed into naming your Ikigai. I expect most readers are either still completely unsure of what their Ikigai might be, or deeply questioning whether they've "done it right" at this point in the book. And that's perfectly fine.

Instead of harping on the meaning of life and your reason for living, let's take a moment to step back and consider why you're going on this journey in the first place.

Ask yourself a few questions, and be gentle with the answers:

- Why am I looking for a reason to live?

- What do I think will change in my life once I've found my Ikigai?

- What kind of comfort will I get from having my Ikigai?

You may not have answers to these questions right away. After all, many humans work all day to make money so they and their families can eat and have a secure home. You may think it's a luxury to even stop and think about these questions. But it's not. Please understand that working to balance your mind and your emotions is a step in self-care that is beneficial to you and everyone in your world.

You don't need to become a mountaintop hermit to properly ponder these questions, but I do want you to think about them seriously for a bit. If you want, you can even write them in a journal for later consideration.

So go ahead and ask yourself these questions. Again, don't judge yourself for the answers:

- What kind of things would I need to do to successfully incorporate the concept of Ikigai into my life right now?

- How much time and energy can I devote toward developing my personal philosophy right now?

- Will this stress me out more than it will help me right now?

Many of us feel that the "best" way to do something is "very quickly and as hard as possible." This is simply impossible when it comes to changing something like your personal mindset.

If you were not raised or conditioned with the concept of Ikigai, it likely won't create an automatic life change. It's meant to be a subconscious connection, but sometimes things become very, very subconscious—and by "subconscious", I mean "essentially forgotten."

How do you feel when you make a mistake or forget to do something? If you are very busy right now, you might not have the ability to really connect with your Ikigai right now. The good news is that any meditation or conscious awareness of your reason for living is "good enough." You don't have to fully commit to a 20 Day Plan or follow a rigorous training schedule.

Shifting your perspective can trigger new thoughts and change your life. That may even be why you're reading this book to begin with. It's okay to put deep pursuits like this on a back shelf until you are mentally, emotionally, and physically in a good place to accept the results.

At the same time, the old phrase "there's never a good time" also applies. Changing your mind can be harder than changing physical habits. In fact, many people feel the psychological components of addiction are harder to challenge than the physical aspects.

To offset this potential mental conflict, let's try a little brainstorm. What do you expect your life to look like if you connect with a reason for living?

Some things to consider here include:

- Do you think you'll live longer?

- Do you feel you'll live with a greater purpose?

- Do you believe you'll get more enjoyment out of life?

- Are you hoping to feel more connected to the world around you?

- Are you looking for something to help you fight through a situation you're struggling with?

*There is no wrong answer.* The more truthful you are, the greater your chances of actually reaching those expectations.

Now it's time to play a game of "Spot the Differences." I have always loved this game—even as a young child, I remember delighting in my search for the tiny discrepancies on the drawings in children's magazines and restaurant menus.

Think of your life now. Think of some of the situations you've been through recently. They don't have to be traumatic situations—go right ahead and include something mundane or happy.

Now think of how you would have approached that situation if you were more connected with your reason for living. A word of caution here: it's never helpful to replay situations and conversations over and over again, so don't re-enact the scene line by line.

Just think about how you felt as that scene played out. Maybe you started out apprehensive, then received good news, which surprised you and made you feel joyful.

What would you expect to happen in this scene if you had a closer understanding of your Ikigai?

Ultimately, your goal in this exercise is to uncover why and at what level you are currently looking to interact with the concept of Ikigai.

Know that these values may fluctuate with time. Sometimes giving yourself a complete mental health makeover sounds like a great idea, and other days, just reading this book may be a daunting task. That's okay. Every big project starts with a tiny idea, so let yourself think about what kind you expect from Ikigai for as long as it takes to move you into a deeper connection.

Next, let's connect the concept of Ikigai with your daily lifestyle. Regardless of whether you choose to incorporate Ikigai into your career path or not, we all need to have financial resources of some sort. Most of us rely on some type of job or profession that provides us with an income. And in more cases than not, that job ends up taking a lot of our time and causing a lot of stress.

Let's take a look at Ikigai and living in the hectic modern world—can these two concepts actually live in harmony?

# IKIGAI AND DOING WHAT YOU LOVE

You've probably heard the saying, "Do what you love, and you'll never work a day in your life." While there are a few holes in that logic, the sentiment behind it can be true when practicing Ikigai. Within the concept of Ikigai, you are encouraged to approach every task with the same level of appreciation for not only the outcome but the task itself.

How often do you end your day feeling completely depleted of energy? How many of your daily tasks get your full attention? If you're being completely honest with yourself, are there a few additional aspects of your life that you should pay more attention to?

For some of us, the idea of a long life can be challenging, because we know how difficult getting through each day can be. That can even be the case for residents of those fabled Blue Zones, who often continue doing their jobs as long as possible. While some people may feel their career is their Ikigai, there are just as many people who consider their job nothing more than a way to put food on the table.

Is Ikigai a way to discover your dream job? It can be. The four-circle diagram would lead us to believe that our reason for living and our purpose in life are the same.

It can also be a way to find something to look forward to in your life, even if your current job is tedious. While Ikigai can't make your paycheck bigger, your boss nicer, or your coworkers less irritating, it can help you accept and appreciate your current situation. The Five Pillars of Ikigai encourage us to reflect inward and connect to ourselves honestly in order to find a way to harmoniously connect with our own lives instead of relying on external motivation.

The different expressions of Ikigai can be applied to many aspects of our lives, whether we use this practice to help guide our career goals, or as a reminder that our existence extends beyond our daily jobs.

## Passion, Mission, Vocation, and Profession in the Modern World

Remember these words? These words appeared at the meeting points of the circles in the Winn/Zuzunaga diagram. You may have noticed that there are also a few areas where the circles overlap that did not receive labels. Interestingly enough, if you search for this diagram online, you'll find that many experts have created their own interpretations of what these areas symbolize. As a result, the terms passion, mission, vocation, and profession may have slightly different contextual meanings in various versions of this diagram.

In many instances, we would consider these words synonyms. These labels were created to represent significant overlap in concepts, as well. But in this context, they are slightly different:

- **Passion** means something you cannot live without. Whatever it is, it would be in your life in some capacity no matter what. You don't just love your passion—you're actually pretty good at it.

- Your **mission** is the way in which you can benefit your community. You have an internal drive to provide your input here. The world needs you, your thoughts, and your actions in this context.

- **Vocation** is a different sort of service. As the meeting place of what the world is looking for and what has monetary value in the Venn diagram, this is commonly thought of as what you do for money, regardless of your emotional connection to that activity.

- Finally, **profession** indicates proficiency—particularly, a level of understanding that makes an individual outstanding in their field. Not only are you quite good at this talent, but it has value within the community.

There is some argument about whether "what you can get paid for" in the diagram means actual monetary payment. Many experts feel that your reason for living shouldn't have a monetary component. Some redefine "payment" to mean "can provide benefit to others and inspire a reciprocal relationship." Since community is at the heart of Ikigai, both definitions are pretty reasonable.

One important takeaway from the diagram is that everything, *everything* that appears in the circles is a good and worthy thing to write down. There are so many stigmas associated with different jobs, and some people who have completed this exercise note that they felt ashamed of some of their answers.

Again, this is not a binding contract, but rather a brainstorming session. The words that arise when contemplating each of these areas of your life can be used as launch pads for bigger ideas—just like we learned earlier, talking about ice cream and dogs. If you dig deeper into how much you really love your passion, you might find greater potential for a profession than you originally thought. For each idea you have, another one will surely follow if you give it time and careful consideration.

Furthermore, the values you might use in each circle can change. We all go through phases where we find ourselves immersed in a popular television show, or can't stop listening to a brand new album. Maybe you've experienced New Book Syndrome, in which you simply cannot put the new release down until you're done—no spoilers here!

Before you head down a committed career path that involves a significant investment of time, money, and overall health, it's important to consider whether you're pursuing your Ikigai, or just running toward the first word that makes logical sense.

Holding onto a goal or routine simply because you identified it as Ikigai is about as wise as holding onto a candle as it burns down past your fingers. Let go of whatever does not serve you, but take time to adjust your gaze. There may be more than one possibility lurking in each of these overlapping areas.

## Using Ikigai to Bring Career Focus: a True Story

A friend of mine once shared a story about her reason for living, and how the most obvious path to her Ikigai turned out to be the wrong path.

As long as she can remember, my friend Brenda has loved animals. From livestock to exotics and housepets, she always develops a certain bond with the animals she encounters.

In turn, animals like her! She's ended up assisting her pets' veterinarians on many occasions, and she's the type of woman stray or lost animals will approach. Brenda has volunteered in animal rescue and had a soothing way with the animals.

For many years, her friends and family encouraged her to pursue veterinary training. After all, she loves it and she's good at it, as well as satisfying the questions of "What the world needs" and "What you can get paid for".

Seems pretty obvious, right?

So, Brenda applied to vet tech school as a first step. She loved what she was learning. She also got a job as a receptionist at a veterinarian's office, and that's where she discovered her main challenge: People.

While my friend loves working with animals, and animals enjoy being in her presence, the pets who visit a veterinarian's office are accompanied by their humans. These humans are frequently scared, angry, overwhelmed, confused, or otherwise emotional when taking their pet in for medical concerns. It turned out my friend Brenda didn't have the same connection with other humans as she did with their furry friends.

At first, she said she felt ashamed and confused. Veterinary medicine was supposed to be her reason for living. She couldn't imagine a world without animals, she felt confident in her skills and talents, and her abilities were definitely useful, helpful, and necessary.

Her perceived failure impacted her life in a very negative way. She assumed she wasn't as good with animals as she thought. She decided she was the problem. She hadn't tried hard enough. If sh kept working at it, maybe she could perfect this vet thing.

In reality, she was simply focused in the wrong direction. Shortly after she resigned from the vet receptionist job, Brenda ended up advertising her services as a pet sitter in her community bulletin. She received a call from one client, then another. Both were thrilled to learn that she had a background in veterinary medicine as well as experience with so many different creatures.

These clients recommended Brenda's service to other individuals, and from that one ad in the community bulletin, Brenda now has a pretty substantial list of pet-sitting clients. She's booked years in advance for gigs lasting days, weeks and even months.

In my friend's case, it wasn't that she was wrong. *She* wasn't the problem. Animals, caring for animals, and helping others care for their animals were all part of her reason for being. It's just that she needed a slight adjustment to her gaze. Brenda is far more comfortable working with one family, farm, or facility at a time rather than interacting with dozens of emotional people every day.

There are millions of stories like Brenda's, and that's why I want to remind you that the exercises you do regarding Ikigai are intended to bring you closer to answers. It might take you a few tries to figure out exactly how the pieces of the diagram come together, but with patience and understanding, they can begin to take shape.

## Ikigai, Doing What You Love, and Sustainable Employment

You've likely also heard the phrase "If you can't have the job you want, love the job you have." In this mindset, those who don't necessarily have their dream career are encouraged to redirect their enthusiasm to whatever income opportunity they have.

But trying to put your heart and soul into a job that you don't care for can make it even more stressful than it needs to be. Why burn yourself out trying to achieve perfection at a job you don't care about?

Within the framework of Ikigai, this phrase looks a little different. The pursuit of perfection is redirected into a delight in constantly noodling away at your favorite task. The need to please others is replaced by the concept of contributing to the community. Within Ikigai, it's not about feeling that you have done the best possible job so much as that the work you have done has made an impact on the lives of those around you.

So who does your work impact? Regardless of what kind of job you have, someone's day is affected by how well you perform as you work.

Let's say you're an office cleaner. If you didn't show up every day, trash cans in that office would start overflowing. The bathrooms would get more disgusting every day. First the offices and then all the common areas would start to smell terrible. All sorts of insects would decide the trash cans are just perfect to raise a family. People might start getting sick. Though there might be days when you feel like you "just" clean offices, the way you do your job impacts everyone in that office, their families, their clients, and even their clients' families.

Perhaps you work in a role where you don't feel that your work has any value to anyone outside your place of employment. That might be true, but think of the impact your work has on those who work within the same environment. By doing your job, you are providing an important piece of the product, service, or industry in which you work. The decisions you make and how well you do your job always impacts someone else.

That's true even for something as simple as an assembly line. Alice puts the first piece on the line. Bob looks over Alice's work and adds a second piece. Carol looks over Alice and Bob's work and adds a third piece, and so on until the object has been fully built.

But what if Alice put the first piece on the line ever so slightly off-center? And then to compensate, Bob had to tighten the second piece a little tighter than usual? So then Carol has to either halt the project altogether—usually with harsh consequences—or come up with yet another way to compensate for all of the collective corrections that have been made so far.

So while you may feel that your role in a corporate environment doesn't actually matter to the customer or end user of your business, that notion is false. What you did enabled someone else to succeed, which in turn created opportunities for better options, which resulted in an overall improved experience for the consumer.

The problem is, we don't always acknowledge how much importance we each have within our roles.

In an August 2017 BBC article regarding Ikigai and the workplace, the CEO of HR consulting firm Jinzai Kenkyusho, Toshimitsu Sowa is quoted as saying, "In a culture where the value of the team supersedes the individual, Japanese workers are driven by being useful to others, being thanked, and being esteemed by their colleagues."

The spirit of community extends, therefore, not just to those who share your village or city, but to all those who are included within your day-to-day life. Within the context of Ikigai, having meaning in your life will allow you to focus on ways to create a positive impact for everyone you interact with.

## Getting Paid Versus Doing What You Love

For many of us, however, it's hard to reconcile what you would really love to do with your current reality. You may wish with every part of your being to be a neurologist. However, becoming a neurologist requires extensive education. This can require a decade of study, and thousands of dollars in university tuition. Not everyone can drop everything and run off to study to become a neurologist just because their Ikigai diagram told them they should.

Where you live can also have an impact on your employment prospects. Maybe your Ikigai chart shows you should be involved with marine biology... but you live in Wyoming. Perhaps you live in a small or rural community with very few opportunities, and moving to even a nearby city is out of the question. You may know exactly where you need to be in order to succeed in the future foretold by your Ikigai questionnaire, but you are either unable or unwilling to uproot your life right this second.

If this were a less honest piece, I would tell you to follow your dreams no matter what, because that's the only way to truly be happy. I don't believe that though, because it simply isn't true.

This book isn't a precise, exacting blueprint that needs to be submitted to the inspectors before you can put it into action. It's more like a sketch of a map, hastily scribbled on the back of a diner menu. It's intended to be a lifelong journey, not a quick fix.

So maybe you don't quit your current job and apply to medical school. But you do start looking at the study material for the medical school entrance exam. You don't tear up your backyard to make an herb garden and become a wellness guru, but you research beneficial plants that suit your area. The idea is to take a low-risk step towards understanding the true direction in which your Ikigai is pointing you.

Your Ikigai should answer questions like:

- Why am I doing the job/living in the place that I am currently?

- What am I looking forward to?

- What would be the ideal situation for me?

- What can I do that would inspire my passion to do it every day?

- What is it that I want to achieve in my life?

What you're doing now may not directly align with what you want to be doing some day, but that doesn't mean you can't continually look for new opportunities that might help you refine or come even closer towards your purpose.

For better or worse, our circumstances can change with no warning. When searching for Ikigai, keep in mind that it is not the pursuit of perfect success in the sense that you must do everything possible to make your dreams come true, but the gentle and purposeful act of working on something because doing so completes your life.

As you experience changes and opportunities, ask yourself the questions above. You might not be exactly where you hoped to be, but that place can certainly be the stepping stone to something else.

If you are struggling with a wide gap between "doing what you love" and "getting paid what you need in order to survive," you are not alone. You are not doing Ikigai improperly, and you should not give up. Like my friend Brenda, adjust your focus. Consider what you are trying to achieve and let your quest for your Ikigai guide your actions.

## What You're Good at Vs. What People Need

Everyone has a talent. In fact, I'm convinced that everyone has more than a few tricks up their sleeves. From curling your tongue to reciting the alphabet backwards, everyone has a few unusual abilities.

Interestingly enough, many people refer to these abilities as "stupid tricks" or "useless talents." They feel that there's no benefit in being able to make faces with exaggerated expressions or being able to memorize and recite a long list of letters.

Granted, these are not highly marketable job skills at first glance. But try digging deeper—why do you make faces? Because it helps people feel engaged with the stories you tell? Because people laugh in appreciation? Having a sense of humor, connecting with others, and wanting to make people feel happy are all admirable traits.

And if you can memorize 26 letters, what else can you memorize? Nearly every career or educational opportunity requires some form of memory skills—whether it's remembering computer code, menu options, paint colors, or your clock-in password.

If you find you have a knack for something, don't automatically dismiss it just because you don't think it's relevant to any future goals. Earlier we discussed the concept of doing things with the purpose of creating a positive impact in someone else's world. This is one such example—just because your silly faces haven't earned you an Academy Award, it doesn't mean they're useless.

Try to consider how you might incorporate the things you do very well into the things you do every day:

- How does the way you do these things help you excel?

- How would you rate your confidence level when you do these things? Does it rise or fall?

- How do you feel inside when you're good at something?

- What are some ways you can incorporate these skills into your daily routine?

You may also underestimate how much what you do is appreciated. What makes you feel grateful in your day-to-day life? Perhaps the staff who served you at a restaurant smiled at you and sincerely wished you a good day when you were feeling down. Maybe your coworker called at just the right time and saved the day. It doesn't have to be earthshaking to be a cause for gratitude—and the little things you do every day may be the reason someone else feels grateful. Be proud of your skills, regardless of whether you feel the world needs them or not. Consider all of the wonderful things that have happened today, even if all that happened is that your needs were met.

Gratitude is an important aspect of Ikigai. Feeling thankful for our existence, for our experiences, and for our relationships can help us find healthful balance and guide us toward a future-facing focus.

Think of the impact you have on others, and that others may have on you. This isn't as much about harsh words and criticism, as it is about the little things that impacted your overall well-being.

These things, however insignificant they may seem in dollar amount, visibility, or direct impact, are the expressions of Ikigai. The meaning of life is the joy of the pursuit, not necessarily the size of the paycheck.

The sad truth is that many of us are discouraged from dwelling on talents that don't seem directly related to making money or having a stable career. Instead of completely walking away from these talents, what if you worked to incorporate them into your present and future?

When we feel unappreciated and distracted by things that have nothing to do with our reason for living, it can make it seem like we haven't really found the meaning of life after all. You may feel like having a reason to wake up every morning might work for some people, but not for you. You might have too much proof that your dreams will never come true, or that having goals is for silly people who don't subscribe to reality.

It's true—there is no guarantee your dreams will come true. But what if you did as much as you could, whenever you could, to get as close to your dream as possible? If your Ikigai is career-related, you might try reframing this from a goal to a pursuit. You Ikigai is to continually improve yourself, not be the best that ever was.

Furthermore, your Ikigai doesn't have to be related to your career at all. While many of us connect our reason with living with the career path we choose, let's look at how an Ikigai that reflects a relationship, routine, or ritual can impact the work you do.

## Directing Desire and Everyday Ikigai

Within Ikigai exists a permission to indulge in what you love, as well as a commitment to exercise discipline within this indulgence. It is a balance of abandoning oneself in the pleasure of purpose while recognizing the needs that still exist beyond your focal point.

Ikigai is not obsession. When a person is obsessed with something, they appreciate that object (or person) to an unhealthy level. They disregard cultural, ethical, and even legal principles in order to indulge their addiction. Despite any logical understanding they may have about their thoughts and actions, they are unable to control themselves.

Within the concept of Ikigai, there is structure, compassion, and a childlike sense of curiosity. You are not looking to overcome, control, or master your Ikigai. Instead, there is gratitude—you are thankful for the opportunity to have a deep and meaningful life.

But as several experts have noted, Ikigai isn't necessarily connected to a skill or a paycheck.

How did you feel when you read Nakanishi's statement, "This child is my Ikigai?" You might have felt moved. Perhaps there is a special person in your life who is largely your objective for moving forward.

You might be a little confused right now—how could any of this possibly relate to your job? Should you make sure that your career path is centered around this special relationship? Should you only do work that they approve of, or that could potentially benefit them? Are you supposed to be thankful for the opportunity to simply support another person?

Not exactly. Remember that Ikigai is your reason for living, not for working. Regardless of how stressful or time-consuming it is, work is only a part of your life.

Sure, your job takes up a lot of your day. But not your whole day. If you love your work—if it's your Ikigai—then dive in and pursue it with all your heart. But if your Ikigai is something or someone else, don't stress. We tend to focus a lot on how our jobs can benefit our lives, but what if we considered instead how our life could benefit our jobs?

Focusing on a beloved child or family member could inspire you to make choices that uplift and strengthen them. Whether that's financial support, or scheduling your work so that you can spend the most possible time with that individual, your devotion to your Ikigai—your reason for living—can manifest in the job you choose.

That same focus can also impact how you do your job. Your desire to provide a stable life for this individual may lead you to accepting extra shifts, or doing your best to excel in your role so that you may earn more pay or responsibility. You may develop a dedicated work ethic in order to ensure this person has everything they need. When times become stressful at your job, your focus on this person can help you see there's a bigger picture than an agitated customer or a frustrating boss.

But what if your Ikigai is a ritual, like a morning cup of coffee?  Ken Mogi describes the virtue of appreciating the small things this way: *No matter where you are in the world, if you make a habit of having your favourite things sooner after you get up, for example, chocolate and coffee, dopamine will be released in your brain, reinforcing actions getting up prior to the receipt of the reward.*

- *Awakening Your Ikigai: How the Japanese Wake Up to Joy and Purpose Every Day*

Plenty of us love our coffee, whether that's the morning cup from Starbucks or a leisurely afternoon at the little local coffee shop.  Sure, it keeps us awake—but how can little rituals like coffee actually impact your career success?

Here we return to the concept of balance.  Let's follow the example Mogi set and say that when you wake up, the first thing you do is start brewing something hot while you take a shower.  With your tea steeping or your coffee brewing, you have just a few steps to follow between the first moment your eyes open and the moment your day truly begins.

Maybe the alarm goes off and you are filled with dread, just like we talked about at the beginning of this book.  You might have a hard day ahead of you, full of important decisions and cranky customers, not to mention dozens of surprises you can't begin to predict.

You don't have control over customers and surprises, and everyone has to make heavy-hitting decisions on a daily basis.  That's just the way life goes, even if you're a seasoned and serene Ikigai practitioner.  What you do have control over, however, is the time that belongs to you.  Let's take a look at this scenario again, and how it might play out if that morning ritual was your Ikigai:

The alarm goes off. You feel startled. Then anxious. You're grumpy. That's perfectly normal—they're called "alarms" for a reason.

But you keep moving through this emotional fog.  You make your way to the kettle or the coffeemaker.  You pour the exact amount of all the ingredients necessary to make your favorite morning drink.  You've practiced this over and over, experimenting with different amounts of this or that. Sometimes you like a little extra sweetness; other times you like it iced rather than hot.

You take your time, not rushing, because you have set aside enough time to complete this ritual in a way that is comforting and enjoyable. You are familiar with the process and know exactly where you can cut corners if you need to save a little time. But you don't really need to—after so much practice, much of the preparation is based on muscle memory.

Despite the taxing day that may await you, you step into the shower once your beverage is in progress. The water is exactly the right temperature, and because you do this every day, you've remembered to have a soft, fluffy towel waiting exactly where you need it when you're done. Well, maybe you forgot today, but that's alright. Now you have a reason to remember tomorrow!

You've got your favorite bathing products on hand, so everything feels, smells, and looks right when you're done. Maybe you've taken the time to choose an outfit that reflects how you feel today, but that doesn't necessarily have to be part of your routine.

Once you're ready, it's time to appreciate your beverage. It should be ready by now. You notice the temperature of it. The scent fills your nose, making you feel at home. You might take a moment to appreciate the color or texture of your beverage before you taste it.

This is your time. Your Ikigai is this ritual, which allows you to fill your senses with simple pleasure. Perfecting this ritual makes you feel complete. You look forward to the sense of balance it brings you. In this moment, you can contemplate the day ahead, prepare for what may be coming, or meditate.

Not the contemplative type? That's fine. Your ritual doesn't have to be peaceful, either. While a low-dopamine morning encourages saving your energy, maybe *your* special ritual helps you get pumped up. You might dance or do yoga to get the blood flowing and connect with your body before your day gets started.

Or maybe it's not a "first thing in the morning" type of situation. Maybe your reason for living is something you do at the end of the day, like the bedtime rituals discussed earlier.

In either case, looking forward to your Ikigai is what gets you through the stresses of the day.

Your Ikigai might not lead you to your ultimate vocation. Remember, the "what people need" and "what you can get paid for" aspects of the chart are not inherent in the traditional practice of Ikigai.

Connecting Ikigai with the workplace is more than finding your dream job– it's about incorporating what you love and do well into every task at hand. What you love and what you're good at don't have to be the same as what people need and what you can get paid for, but you might enjoy what you get paid for more if your work is connected to your Ikigai, regardless of whether your job is related to your reason for living or not.

The relationship between the constant pursuit of your meaning of life has been likened to a type of perfection. But the perfection of Ikigai isn't one-and-done perfection like a flawless computer program, or even the gold medalist atop the platform. It's perfection like the natural growth of a tree or the flow of a river current. This pursuit involves a regular devotion to refining your process. Focus on the positive impact of the actions you have taken today, and how what you have done has paved the way for others.

Ikigai is not an obsession. It is not a competition. There is no prize for winning, and there is no punishment if you don't reach your goals. There is just the satisfaction of knowing you have the opportunity to connect with this goal, motivation, or ritual for the rest of your life.

It is also highly unlikely that your Ikigai will magically reveal itself to you in absolute clarity. Even after completing all of the exercises in this book, you may still feel like you're gazing at the answer through several layers of distorted glass. The vision you get will become clearer as long as you keep your focus on it.

Reflecting on your Ikigai from a work standpoint, you might find yourself feeling frustrated by how close or far away you feel from it. You might feel that it's too difficult to connect with your Ikigai due to your current location or situation. You might also find yourself wishing you didn't have to work so you could spend more time concentrating on your Ikigai.

These feelings are legitimate and can make it difficult to really connect with your Ikigai. You might just give up on the concept of there being a bigger purpose to your life. But remember—your Ikigai doesn't have to be a big money earner. Your Ikigai is ultimately a lifelong pursuit, and can have as much or as little influence on your career as you wish to coordinate.

It can be difficult to think beyond some of the more obvious options, but as my friend Brenda demonstrated, a closer connection to your Ikigai may reveal choices to you that you didn't even know existed. Unfortunately, very few of us have the opportunity to experiment with our career. That doesn't mean, though, that you should abandon your dreams—and you definitely shouldn't be walking away from something as important as your reason for living!

Sometimes, in order to fully understand what options surround us, we need to allow all possibilities to exist—"however improbable," to borrow the words of Sherlock Holmes. If we ignored real-life limitations during the brainstorming process, what might your reason for living look like?

## Exercise Four: What Would You Do If You Could Do Absolutely Anything?

For many of us, practicality tends to have a strong hold on us—even when we're daydreaming. But this isn't a question for practicality—at least, not yet.

In this exercise, you'll find a series of questions intended to help you concentrate on what you love and what you excel at without worrying about the practicality or career impact of these things.

You might be wondering why an exercise that asks you to ignore the career aspect of Ikigai would be used in a chapter about Ikigai and how you make a living. But in this exercise, you'll probably find out one of two things:

1. Your Ikigai is closely related to your career goals and future planning

2. Your Ikigai is a ritual, a connection, a relationship, or journey

You will also have the opportunity to surprise yourself. Try to take the questions one at a time and really consider your answers. Answer each question without any additional context. Answer it completely. Depending on the type of thinker you are, you might want to think about the question for several days, or you might want to jot down the first things that come to mind, depending on the type of thinker you are.

While "yes, but" statements aren't entirely conducive to this exercise, it's still important to identify and address your fears—which we'll do more in an additional exercise. You might want to scribble these down so you can remember them later, but it's best not to dwell on them here. They'll have a purpose later.

As you prepare for this exercise, you may wish to start by reflecting on Ken Mogi's Five Pillars again:

- *Pillar 1: Starting small*

- *Pillar 2: Releasing yourself*

- *Pillar 3: Harmony and sustainability*

- *Pillar 4: The joy of little things*

- *Pillar 5: Being in the here and now*

In discussing Ikigai and work, you might feel stressed, confused, maybe even defeated. What is the source of that worry? For many people, it is the dissonance between a dream and reality. Few of us are living the life of our dreams. But remember—Ikigai is a reason for living, not a dream come true.

When making plans, we all know that there will be challenges along the way. That knowledge is enough to keep some people from trying to reach their goals in the first place.

But what if our resources were limitless, and we didn't have to worry about the practicality of anything? What if we only thought about "would" and not "could"?

Ideally, practitioners of Ikigai would continuously—and eventually subconsciously—apply Mogi's pillars to their daily lives. It will take you many years of dedication to get to that point, so for now, use your current understanding of each pillar to help you achieve this mindset. In fact, you may wish to revisit these questions from time to time to see whether your perspective has changed.

What if you were to start small? What if, when considering your Ikigai, you really did let all of the thoughts come out? We've talked about examples that might seem silly, like ice cream and playing with dogs, but when brainstorming what you love, it's generally the most insignificant things that will come to mind first. Too often, we're willing to say, "Oh, that's dumb," and ignore an idea. What if we acted in a child-like way and didn't dismiss every idea, just because it might not be logical, productive, or practical?

Then, what if you released all of your misconceptions about yourself? What if you let the real you drive, instead of whatever mask you're wearing at the moment? None of us want to acknowledge that anything is wrong in our lives or that we are anything less than 100% at all times. I admit, everyone has to "fake it to make it" from time to time. But the more you force yourself to tolerate less-than-ideal situations, the less willing you will be in the long term to consider other opportunities. You might decide that trying to connect with your meaning of life is foolish or a waste of time because you'll only end up disappointed.

But the fact that you are searching for your reason for living in any capacity shows that you are interested in this type of change, and that you feel connecting with your Ikigai might provide some benefit to your overall well being.

So please, take a few moments to really think about the importance of finding joy in little things before you start answering these questions. Think about *your* favorite "little things", whether that's the perfect blanket that you snuggle under at bedtime or a pretty patch of land on your morning commute. Continue to apply that pure level of unbiased appreciation as you work through this exercise.

Once you find yourself in that open and relaxed state, allow yourself to honestly answer the following questions. You can write down your answers, journal about your thoughts, or whatever feels like the best option to help you work through the puzzle.

- *What never fails to make you smile?*

- *What is something that you never get bored with?*

- *If you never had to worry about money again, how would you spend most of your time?*

- *What activity always makes you feel excited?*

- *What kind of compliments do you typically get from your peers? Your family? Your friends?*

- *Which task at any job you've had is your favorite, and why?*

- *If you were asked to teach a small group of people a skill, which skill would you choose?*

- *What types of chores or tasks feel really easy to you?*

- *What do you want to achieve in life?*

- *How do you want to be remembered?*

- *What were you doing the last time you had so much fun, you lost track of time?*

As you answer these questions, try to think of specific answers. Perhaps you can call up memories or specific examples that relate to each question. Take some time to recollect the experience or feeling you had at the time.

For example, here's my answer to the question "*Which task at any job you've ever had is your favorite, and why?*"

Once upon a time, I worked in a small bakery. I loved working the front-of-house closing shift best—the bakers took care of their area in the back. I really enjoyed cleaning up all the messes from the day, restoring order in the customer-facing area, and getting everything ready to go for the hectic opening shift. The process of taking everything from sticky, icing-smeared chaos to a neat, tidy, and quaint bakery was soothing to me. I loved dismantling the day's displays, cleaning them, and reassembling so they would be ready for the morning shift. Being able to see the difference my efforts made was really satisfying to me.

Today, I get the same feeling when a draft comes back from my brilliant editors. Though there is a screen full of brightly-colored markups staring back at me, I see opportunities to improve and reorganize.

As I wrote this, I could remember all of the sights, sounds, smells, feelings, and even tastes from working at the bakery. I thought of the way I had to use a plastic knife to get all of the pecan roll caramel off of the display trays. Or how we would run leftover bagels through the bread slicers to make croutons—which we would happily snack on while cleaning the counters and espresso machine.

See if you can answer these questions in that level of detail. You might want to jot down some of the thoughts and memories that come to mind as you do so. You might even have emotions or questions, and this is a great opportunity to explore them further!

For the life of me, I can't understand why I was so obsessed with chiseling all of the hardened caramel off the tray—the bakers were constantly offering to take care of it before they set up the display. While I wouldn't say that attacking sugar with a plastic utensil is my Ikigai, there are clearly some things I need to meditate on when it comes to what I love and what I'm good at. Maybe there's an opportunity in that behavior that I can apply elsewhere in my life.

This exercise should encourage you to connect the dots between your passion, your mission, your profession, and your vocation. No, you don't have to become a professional at your strange and obscure talent... but what is it about that strange and obscure talent that benefits your existence? And to take it one step further, how can your continued practice of that strange and obscure talent keep your health in balance by settling your mind, emotions, and body?

Barb's Story

Slowly, Barb's daily journal time expands. She sips her coffee, writes whatever comes to mind, and savors the silence. She writes stories from raising a family, memories of her own childhood, a few tales from her long career.

She tucks the handwritten pages away in their own drawer, but copies all her entries into an impeccably coded and cross-referenced file. Maybe Becky or Becky's daughter will want a copy someday.

While writing, she remembers a sweet moment from Timothy's childhood. She drafts an email to tell him about it, deletes it, and tries two more times before finally sending it. It's nothing stunning, just an old story that makes her smile. Maybe it won't, and then she'll try again later. Like perfection, reconciliation is a pursuit and not a binary switch.

That daily hour of serenity keeps Barb going. She doesn't know for sure if this is her Ikigai. But it's a signpost along the way. And for the first time in years, Barb looks forward to waking up tomorrow morning.

# CONCLUSION

Discovering your Ikigai, your reason for living, your purpose in life, or the meaning of life—however you prefer to frame it, you are embarking on a lifelong quest.

You probably have a ton of questions, starting with "so now what?" While I wish there was a blanket answer I could share, the answer really is different for everyone.

In fact, you might consider your Ikigai the answer to that question. Now what? Now you find yourself one step closer to your reason for living. What do you do after that? Find a way to get even closer. And closer.

In Ikigai, "close" doesn't mean "on the brink of success." It suggests an emotional closeness, as in "I am close to my brother but closer to my parents." It is an intimacy or appreciation.

There are also many readers who haven't really figured out their Ikigai yet. That's okay—this isn't a race to have your reason for living completely sorted out before the last page. As a matter of fact, I have included a few additional exercises to help you in your ongoing journey.

Over time, you may feel that you have drawn away from your Ikigai. That is not a sign that you're doing it wrong and should completely give up on what you once considered your reason for living. In fact, it might be a sign that you're more closely connected than you believed.

Your Ikigai may or may not change over time. If something does happen to drastically impact your relationship with your Ikigai, it doesn't necessarily mean you should abandon it altogether. As we've discussed, your gaze upon your Ikigai may be ever-changing, depending on your circumstances.

Whether you're unsure about your Ikigai, or find yourself questioning whether you're approaching it from the right angle, consider revisiting these exercises from time to time. The more you practice any skill, the more appreciation and flair you'll have for it.

Many experts feel that maintaining optimum health is ideal for living a long life, and while there are certainly no guarantees, it is clear that our choices and actions can throw our mental, emotional, and physical health out of balance. The more you focus on your Ikigai, the more you'll appreciate the potential it has for elevating all areas of your life. If balance between mental, emotional, and physical health is the basis for well-being, your connection to your Ikigai can be the blueprints to continually build onto that base.

Those who practice Ikigai likely experience the same traumas and tragedies that you do. They have experienced lousy bosses, terrible work and home situations, loss, anxiety, and depression. They are not impervious to disease or accidents. But their focus keeps them going, turning the stress we all undergo into an obstacle to work around, rather than a force of pure destruction.

Will Ikigai help you achieve outstanding mental health, emotional clarity, and restore your health? It can, but not overnight. You will need to put effort into understanding:

- What your Ikigai is

- How you relate to it

- How to incorporate your reason for living into the stressful moments of the day

- How to appreciate your Ikigai and celebrate the meaning it has in your life, even when life doesn't feel like much of a party

This is not something you can do overnight, or even over a weekend. Those who practice Ikigai do so every day of their lives. Acknowledging and honoring your reason for living should be reflected in the choices you make and the things that you do, but this won't happen instantly.

Imagine if this book were about wearing your pants backwards. You could start wearing your pants backwards the minute you finish reading it, but it probably wouldn't feel comfortable at first. You might struggle with getting them fastened. Sometimes you might forget and put them on the way you used to. Or think of getting a new prescription for glasses. At first they're awkward—they're heavy, they feel strange on your face, you forget to pick them back up when you put them down—but with time and practice, you realize how much clearer everything has become.

Any change is like that. Just because you personally feel pressure to discover your Ikigai and become attached to it as quickly as possible, it doesn't mean that's actually going to happen.

Don't create a scenario for failure. Instead, embrace this as a wonderful opportunity to become more knowledgeable with yourself and your needs.

This is especially true if your Ikigai relates to a specific career path or your connection with your work. You cannot force the world to turn, you cannot cause the sun to rise, and you cannot erase your current circumstances for a dream.

What you can do, however, is allow yourself to embrace each new day. Allow yourself to do things that relate to your passion, mission, profession, and vocation. Let go of any false version of yourself and welcome a sense of childlike wonder as you focus and refocus on the meaning of life. There is no right or wrong path, only opportunity to fulfill your soul, balance your health and well being, and connect with your reason for living.

When the alarm goes off in the morning, your heart may still race. You may lie in bed for a few moments thinking about how great it would be if you could just stay there as long as you wanted. You may take some time bracing yourself for whatever tasks might await you on this new day. You may even grumble as you prepare for a particular situation.

But those who have an Ikigai have a little something extra. They know their reason for living. They know that no matter what, they will be able to do something that day that connects them to their meaning of life. Whether they have a productive day or just do the bare minimum, they have had an opportunity to participate in their own life, community and world.

And with that peace of mind, they continue, day after day, for the rest of their lives.

Your life may not change dramatically once you finish this book. In fact, I would expect it to be entirely coincidental if that were the case! However, if you take one thing away from our discussion of what it takes to live a long and meaningful life, I hope it is that we each have a long way to go to fully understand ourselves.

Through the course of this book, you have likely encountered questions you've never considered before. You may have had a change in understanding certain things about yourself, or gotten deeper insight into why you are the way you are. While these are not necessarily part of the Ikigai experience, it simply goes to show what complicated and fascinating creatures we are. We start a journey with one goal in mind, but learn so many lessons along the way.

If you choose to continue your Ikigai journey, the following section includes four exercises that allow for deeper concentration on some of the aspects of Ikigai we've learned about.

I love to write, I love to explore new ideas, and I love to communicate those ideas to others. So as I wish you all the best on your journey, I also thank you all for being a part of my own Ikigai.

# IKIGAI EXERCISES

The following exercises are built on the concept of Ikigai, as well as some of the tenets discussed throughout the book.

As with the previous exercises, these are designed to help you when you find yourself stuck in a concept of Ikigai. Whether you're having trouble connecting to yourself to honestly delve into anything important, or you feel frustrated by the conflict between your dreams and reality, these exercises are designed to direct your thoughts to guide you to a more contemplative state of mind.

You may wish to perform these exercises all at once or piece by piece. I encourage you to take the time to truly consider the questions here. Each is designed so that you can work slowly to come up with honest and thorough answers.

Some of the questions are fun, while others are serious. I encourage you to read each exercise in its entirety before you decide to complete it. Sometimes philosophical contemplation can result in a flood of unpleasant thoughts and memories. The goal of these exercises is to invoke peaceful and thoughtful contemplation, and while that might result in some emotions coming to surface, the overall result should be more informative than upsetting.

If you are not comfortable completing the exercises as they stand, I encourage you to read the concepts of each exercise. Perhaps they'll help you to a richer understanding of why the exercise doesn't feel like such a good idea.

Take care of yourself, and I hope these four additional exercises help you feel more in tune with your reason for living.

## Exercise: Release and Accept Yourself

For many of us, it is difficult to connect with who we are as a person because we have worked hard to establish every version of ourselves. You might be the person who stays late to finish a difficult task at work, the messiest person in the house, the baker of the best chocolate chip cookies, the most efficient dog walker, and the last person anyone should call if there's a spider around. But the way your boss, your coworkers, your mother, and a small child see you may be different. Many of us work very hard to ensure others in our lives receive the version of us that best suits their needs.

In order to understand your Ikigai, it can be helpful to unify all of these different ways of viewing yourself. In this exercise we'll focus less on doing what we feel we should do, and more on thoughts, actions, and ideas that feel authentic to our true selves.

Sometimes, we have trouble telling the objective truth to ourselves about certain topics. We're so afraid of being judged for our actions, we'll rewrite their experience to fit the expectations of others.

Here's an example of how we sometimes edit reality to avoid others thinking poorly of us:

*You had a delicious frozen pizza last night. You worked late, and you didn't feel like cooking or dealing with delivery. You stopped at the store, grabbed a frozen pizza and some necessities, and headed home to relax with dinner and your favorite television show.*

*Unexpectedly, the pizza was absolutely delicious! It wasn't exactly big, either. The show was good, and the food was tasty, so you ended up eating the entire thing.*

*The next day, you're talking to your coworkers about the show, since you're all fans. You mentioned the pizza you ate. "Ugh!" one friend says. "That stuff is so fatty and gross. I hope you didn't eat more than a few bites!"*

*Many of us are culturally taught to feel ashamed of overindulgence, so you would not be alone if you lied and said, "Yeah. Whew! That stuff was rich! Tasty though!" You might vow to never get that pizza again and feel ashamed every time you remember the incident.*

Even though we know logically that other people's opinions of us shouldn't impact what we do or think about ourselves, it hurts to discover these judgments. In the example above, the coworker has no idea what your dietary requirements are, how tired and drained you were, or how much you enjoyed the pizza. Whether you should or should not have eaten the entire thing is none of their business.

So, despite our best efforts to live our authentic lives, we often incorporate the expectations and judgements of others in our assessment of ourselves.

First, let's try a few silly, low-stress questions to help you disengage from the need to provide answers someone else would expect. Let the creative juices start flowing as you answer these.

1. Where have you been that would have been a totally different experience with a huge glass of ice water in one hand?

2. What's the best ice cream topping that hardly anyone knows about?

3. What's a hobby that you know nothing about?

4. What sport or activity would you like to try, but you've never had the chance?

5. What's a food you'd like to try?

Now let's try a little step towards connecting these questions with your life experiences so far.

1. What moment in your life was really awkward, but everything turned out ok in the end?

2. Do you prefer your ice cream plain, or all dressed up in a sundae, and why?

3. What's a hobby you've been afraid to try?

4. If you were given a blank check, but you were required to spend it on a new hobby or activity, what would you choose?

5. Where is a place you've always wanted to travel?


Do you see how these questions are very similar, yet lead your thoughts in a slightly different direction? The second set of questions allows you to connect with a deeper level of your true likes, dislikes, and emotions.

These baby steps of self-discovery help you connect with your authentic self. At first, you might be hesitant to give a completely honest answer. You might come up with an answer without thinking much about it just for the sake of having the question answered and over with.

If you allow yourself to take baby steps through your own thought process, you'll have a better opportunity to unite with your authentic self. And as you read your answers to these seemingly low-stress questions, you might start thinking "well, actually..." or "it's more like this than that..." Refining your preferences and opinions is part of understanding who you truly are.

For example, you might go further with this set of questions by asking:
1. What do you think you learned from that particular awkward situation?

2. What's something that's far better than ice cream?

3. What do you think would happen if you tried out that scary hobby?

4. How would you get started with your new hobby or activity?

5. What obstacles are in the way of you traveling to that place in the next year/five years/ten years?


Each layer of questioning can inspire you to look deeper into yourself. And though it's pretty unlikely that the answers to any of these questions might be related to your Ikigai, perhaps it's time to adjust your concept of what your Ikigai should be and release yourself to what your Ikigai actually is.

## Exercise: What Aspects of Your Life Need More Attention So You May Thrive?

Wouldn't it be great if all of our needs were met all the time? That healthful equilibrium would be so much easier to maintain, wouldn't it?

Unfortunately, many of us are making do with a little less than we actually need in our lives. That might be time, energy, support, money, or a sense of security. But hardly any of us have everything we need all the time.

When we feel like something is lacking in our lives, we do our best to defend this perceived weakness. We invest extra effort into making sure this frailty isn't discovered. It cannot impede our progress, nor can we let anyone know that there's a potential issue.

Unfortunately, contributing so much of yourself to this task is counter-productive. You feel stress about the problem, and you're struggling to maintain a good facade so that no one knows about it at all.

These problem areas can also have something to do with the roadblocks that have prevented you from successfully pursuing your Ikigai. But what if we allow change to come in a way that incorporates all of the areas in which you feel you might be struggling, rather than considering them to be problems?

Think back to Exercise Two in the main section of the book. We took some time to think about the why and how of connecting to your Ikigai and making important life changes. While discovering your reason for living isn't the same type of struggle as quitting smoking or as deliberate as learning a new language, it is still a major lifestyle update.

Sometimes, change is actually impossible. You can have the best intentions and full motivation, but because of some factor that's out of your hands, you can't give those actions any attention right now.

Other times, we just don't want to give change the attention we know it needs. The timing is inconvenient. It would take too long. It would be too hard. There's too much going on. While some frame these as excuses, there's nothing wrong with acknowledging actual challenges within your life.

Unfortunately, it can be oddly difficult to decide which is the case. We live in a world in which we're expected to power through distress and make do with what we've got, so you may feel that it's a sign of moral weakness to not drop everything and make this change happen with every fiber of your being.

This is not the case. Change happens slowly, and never in a linear fashion.

In this exercise, we'll confront any mental roadblocks that you may have in regard to really connecting with your Ikigai.

To do that, we'll be actively searching through some of our negative emotions. If you are feeling out of balance, or this is not a good time to think about the things about your life that aren't comfortable right now, skip this activity until you're feeling more confident about answering these questions.

While none of these questions are specifically triggering, they do ask questions that require you to be honest about your own feelings and well-being. If now isn't a good time for this type of honesty, choose another exercise for the time being. Working towards balance rarely includes making things even worse.

When you're ready, ask yourself the following questions. I've purposefully phrased these questions so you can answer them from the perspective of "Right now" or "In general."

Perhaps today is a day to focus on one question in particular, or you may find it easier to answer several or all of them at once.

You may even wish to ask yourself these questions sporadically to assess where your mind and heart are at any given moment. Answering these questions may help you reestablish a connection with your Ikigai that has waned or been uncertain lately, too. By connecting with the more negative aspects of your current experience, you might find more ways that your reason for living can give you focus in these trying times.

Ask yourself questions such as:

- *What am I afraid of?*

- *What causes me pain?*

- *What do I need more of right now?*

- *How am I doing mentally?*

- *How am I doing emotionally?*

- *How am I doing physically?*

- *What am I craving?*

But fear not! This exercise is not all about doom and gloom. Instead, it is about connecting your reason for living with your current situation in order to restore balance.

Instead of dwelling on any bad memories or feelings these questions may bring up, now ask yourself these questions:

- *What needs to be addressed to relieve this discomfort?*

- *What are all the things that would need to happen so that you can feel even 1% more connected to your Ikigai?*

- *What is one event that, if it occurred in the next 24 hours, would change your life completely?*

- *What is one action you can do right now that might help your life feel a little more meaningful, despite the challenges you are currently facing?*

Many of us are caught in a cycle of doing the bare minimum to survive. But how would your life look if you attempted to not just survive, but thrive?

Answering these questions—the negative and the positive—can actually help you find a little hope when things seem overwhelming. As discussed in the book, there can be many obstacles preventing us from connecting with our Ikigai in exactly the way we feel we ought to.

That doesn't mean that your reason for living is silly or that your meaning of life is a lie. It means you're going through a rough patch right now where things are out of balance. Completing an exercise like this, in which you admit everything that's going wrong but then brainstorm what it would take to help, can create a little more harmony.

Will knowing what you need actually fix your problems? No—only you can make changes in your own life. However, having a clearer picture of the problem can lead you toward a solution. The more you think about potential solutions, the more glimmers of hope you may find. Even the tiniest action can bring you closer to your own life and your own reason for living.

That glimmer of hope can be fueled by your Ikigai. Whether your Ikigai brings you comfort or provides you with a goal, it can also help you engage your personal resources.

Your appreciation for your natural talents and your acquired skills can give you extra windows to open when you're looking to change your view on a current problem.

Reflect upon and respect the things you need within your life. Consider the things in your control, the things you can change now, and the things that might help you go a little further. If you have the capacity, go ahead and act on them. If you don't, you still know more than you did—and knowledge is power.

## Exercise: Baby Steps—Little Ways You Can Make Your Life More Joyful and Productive

Throughout the book, I've encouraged you to "think further" or "adjust your gaze" in order to find a new way to focus on familiar topics as you search for your Ikigai.

I've also advocated baby steps, or approaching things in a deliberate and detailed way.

Baby steps are so named because they are very small, unsteady, and not necessarily purposeful. Reading this book is a baby step. Taking a look at this exercise is a baby step. Asking yourself these questions, jotting down the answers, and letting yourself brainstorm the impact of those answers—those are all baby steps as well.

There's a lot of work involved in making changes in your life. But just like the pursuit of Ikigai, you don't have to rearrange your entire life all at once.

Think about how you reorganize your living space. I would encourage anyone to start small and to make a plan. As a professional organizer, I recommend individual and business clients alike to consider how they are going to use their space before they commit to changing it. Connecting to your meaning of life and reconciling your lifestyle once that connection has been realized are two different processes.

Little steps may seem painful, but can lead you much further than you believe. Take it slow. Ask for directions. Babies learn to walk through mistakes and practice. So will you.

Sometimes, however, it's hard to keep taking baby steps when you're not sure where you're going. While our first steps don't have much direction, as we keep taking those steps, we eventually walk with a purpose.

I've stated a few times that there is no perfect roadmap for Ikigai, but you can find some of the pieces that might help you put it together within yourself.

In her book *IKIGAI —Giving Every Day Meaning And Joy,* Yukari Mitsuhashi suggests reflecting on your past, present, and future to help you feel more connected with your reason for living.

In this exercise, we're going to use our memories, our ideas, and our plans to help us appreciate what those small glimmers of progress might look like for those who are looking to connect with their Ikigai.

Sometimes, however, when we're meditating on emotional topics like your own memories and experiences, it may be hard to easily organize our thoughts into anything remotely resembling a rational pattern. As the word "trigger" indicates, our memories and emotions may explode beyond our control.

To help you maintain a more productive flow, I've organized some questions into a chart. Concentrate on as much or as little of the chart as you feel comfortable with each time you look at it—again, this isn't a one-and-done kind of exercise.

Think of your Ikigai as a puzzle. You have all of these pieces scattered before you. You know that putting all of the pieces together will help you fully realize your Ikigai, but that's going to take time. You're not sure where everything goes, or what it means. Is your fourth grade rock collection significant, or should you really think about the fact that you make the most refreshing pitcher of lemonade anyone in your family has ever tasted?

While this chart isn't a detailed map, it is a guide that can help you sort through some of the ideas and thoughts that come to mind when you're considering your reason for living.

Based on Yukari Mitsuhashi's recommendation, this chart asks you to consider aspects from your childhood and your current state, while connecting these concepts to your potential future state.

Each question provides you with simple guidance from one thought to another. You may notice that there is no solution state for this chart. Instead, think of it as the top of a waterfall. As your thoughts trickle downward through the questions, allow your ideas to gain momentum. You may actually want additional time to think about your rock collection or excellent lemonade in greater detail. Go right ahead and do that! There's no reason why it might not have bearing on what you discover the meaning of life to be.

I call this chart the "Stepping Stones of Discovering Ikigai." Though I have included several questions to help you consider your past, present and future states of being in terms of your reason for living, these are by no means the only questions you can include here. This is merely an outline to get you started.

I also want you to pay attention to the fact that this is less of a chart than a web. The past, present, and future intertwine on this chart, just as they do in real life.

The dotted arrows in this chart reflect ways in which a thought process may include more than just one period of your life. The things we've learned in our childhood can very clearly impact the way we do things now and the way we plan to do things in the future.

If your thoughts take you from one question to another in a non-linear way, let them. Just as we may discover detours as we navigate through the place where we live, it's always possible to find new connections between our memories, our plans, and what we're doing right this second.

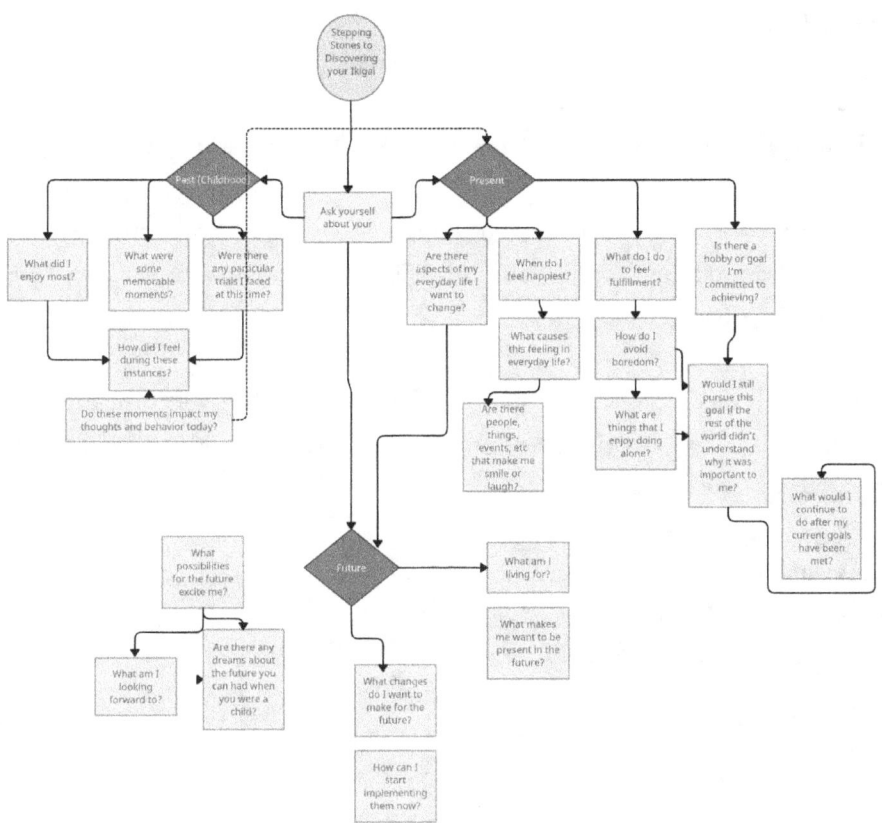

In asking yourself these questions, you may be pointing yourself in a direction that will lead you to a new understanding of your reason for living and why the future is important to you.

## Exercise: Using Your Senses to Search for Your Ikigai

When we work on a project, we start with a vision, and we keep working until we can see that vision come to life.

Finding your Ikigai can be very much like that. This may seem ironic, after I've spent most of the book talking about how Ikigai isn't a one-and-done accomplishment. How can you have a vision for your entire life?  There's no way things would turn out exactly like you planned, anyway!

But dedication, commitment, and understanding all require at least a little vision.  In order to focus ourselves, we need to know what we're looking at at any given time, right?

In this exercise, we're going to use the five senses—vision, hearing, taste, touch, and smell—to help you connect with your daily life.  In doing so, you may find your own Ikigai coming closer into focus.

You may also find more balance within your current well-being as you participate in the here and now.  By consciously engaging the five senses, you may find yourself distracted from the stresses of the day, at least for the moment.

As with every exercise, start small.  Pick up any object close to you.  Now let's use the five senses to really observe it:

- Sight:What color is it?

  ◦ What shape is it?

    • Are there any curves or angles?

    • Does the shape change in any way?

    • Could it be another shape?

  ◦ How big is it?

    • What would it look like if it were bigger?

    • How small could it be before it wouldn't have a purpose?

- Hearing: Does the object make noise or produce sound?

  ◦ Can you make noises by tapping on it?

    • Does it make a sound if you change something about it (such as how a whistle toots when you blow on it)?

- Smell: What does the object smell like?

  ○ Would you want to smell that again?

- Touch: What does the surface of the object feel like?

  ○ Does it move, open, or change?

    - What is that process like?

- Taste: Is this an object that is safe to taste?

  ○ What words would you use to explain how it tastes?

    - Is that what you expected based on the way it looks, feels, and smells?

Now let's take this exercise a step further and apply those same questions and observations from our senses to something that isn't actually in your presence right now. You don't have to make this too abstract or big at first—a good baby step would be asking these questions about something that's just out of the room or that you remember strongly.

The next baby step might be applying these questions to something that might just be your reason for living. What sights do you associate with this goal, person, or ritual? What sounds might be in the background? Set the entire scene in your mind. Are there any particular scents associated with your Ikigai? Someone who connects with marine biology might think of the salty perfume of an ocean breeze, for example. Though you can't necessarily taste or feel the tangible reminders of your Ikigai at this exact moment, recall these sensations as well as you can.

Ikigai involves—and creates—a bond and a dedication. It's a never-ending but peaceful quest for connection and a pursuit to express this zeal.

Connecting to your Ikigai through the physical senses intensifies the existing mental and emotional bond you may have to it. Sure, you know that your morning shower and beverage routine has a place in your mental and emotional well-being. And cleanliness and hydration are important for physical health.

But what about the way the water feels on your skin when you first step in the shower? Or the smell of your coffee mingled with your favorite shampoo? From first sip to last swallow, how was the drink? Do you hear the kettle boil as you prepare it? Or perhaps the sound of the shower running and a glimpse of steam escaping from your bathroom helps you recall your connection to your Ikigai.

Our senses continue working even when we're not consciously focusing on our experiences. You may know your favorite coffee is bitter or sweet, but it's not until you take the opportunity to actually delve into the sensory experience that you can add more notes to this with detailed descriptions like chocolatey, rich, or earthy.

The more you experience something, the more details you notice, and the more details you create. Slowly and surely, each experience leads to the overall purpose of that process in your life. And here, quite possibly, you may be able to find tangible evidence of your Ikigai in what your senses perceive.

With thought and practice, you can instantly recall the sights, sounds, scents, feelings, and tastes of situations and objects you associate with your Ikigai. When you do that, you can carry your Ikigai with you wherever you go.

# REVIEW

Reviews and feedback help improve this book and the author. If you enjoy this book, we would greatly appreciate it if you could take a few moments to share your opinion and post a review on Amazon. Thank you!